WHEN CANCER CLOUDS THE SKY

GOD'S STORY SPOKEN INTO THE LIFE OF ONE FAMILY

Beverly E. Hannah

*"Yet the Lord will command His lovingkindness
in the daytime,
And in the night His song shall be with me,
And my prayer unto the God of my life."
Psalm 42:8*

Copyright 2017 by Beverly E. Hannah, All rights reserved. No part of this book may be used without written permission of the author.

All verses are taken from the King James Version of the Bible.

For additional copies or to contact Bev:
cancercloudsthesky.wordpress.com

Cover Design and Book Printed by
Copyquik
Hagerstown MD 21740

TABLE OF CONTENTS

Acknowledgements

Introduction ... 1

Part One: A Gathering Storm

    I.   No, I Did NOT Break My Hip! ... 9
    II. It's All About Pain! ... 19

Part Two: A Storm in Progress

    III.   The Cancer Journey Begins ... 31
    IV.   Not Our Plans, But His! ... 43
    V.   Everything We Needed To Know When the Journey Began ... 55
    VI.   One More Hurdle Before Treatment? ... 67
    VII. Treatment Begins! ... 81
    VIII. Exciting Moments in the Midst of Uncertainty ... 95
    IX.   Yuck! I Am Stuck in a Trough! ... 111
    X.   When Treatment Ends ... 123

Part Three: A Rainbow Appears

    XI.   What Have We Learned? ... 135
    XII. What's Over the Horizon? ... 143
    XIII. An Afterword ... 151

ACKNOWLEDGEMENTS

Saying "Thank you" is a wonderful privilege. Many friends and family have been instrumental in my getting this book to press, and I would like to offer special thanks to them. A few years have passed since I began writing, so obviously, there have been those who have stepped in and encouraged me to continue when I had taken too long of a break.

When the Lord gives us a spouse, He knows exactly what we will need in the life we spend here on earth. For me, my husband Roger has been the perfect gift, and though he has been a silent partner much of the time, he has nevertheless been the best that anyone could ever ask for! His patience and hours of correcting computer glitches have allowed this project to finally be completed.

Family, too, is special. My sister Jan and our children Roddy and Tonya and their families have endured hours of listening to me read excerpts. Who couldn't love children who never had a critical word about what they were hearing? As I have proofread repeatedly, I have, however, come to realize that perhaps I should have been more welcoming of their evaluation.

Special thanks to my Texas buddy Margaret who initially encouraged the journaling process and to Pastor Sam who has been so eager to offer encouragement and help. There are also countless friends and Pastor Herm who have lent encouragement, sometimes simply by asking, "Have you finished yet?" Thank you to the many who have prayed with and for us through these last years of unexpected challenge.

Finally and most significantly, TO GOD BE THE GLORY! We know He has enabled through His grace thus far, and we know that He continues to work even though the "major" storm cloud has weakened.

INTRODUCTION

"So teach us Lord to number our days that we may apply our hearts unto wisdom."
Psalm 90:12

Sometimes the day dawns bright and beautiful, only to be abruptly interrupted by a severe storm… one that no one even saw coming over the horizon. The sky had been that beautiful azure blue and the threat of a storm seemed to be missing from the radar, and yet the storm came. Life can be the same way! The day dawns calm and peaceful and beautiful, only to be invaded by a sudden and abrupt storm. Sometimes a storm changes the landscape with its vicious winds and rains. Our family has experienced that kind of a storm in our life as a family, and, though the road was often difficult, we have profited from its many distinctly God-given lessons.

We are in the big batch of Christians who consider ourselves to be of the "fairly normal" lot. Husband Roger and I were blessed to be reared in Christian homes. We were high school sweethearts who married after college. In a few years, we were blessed with a daughter Tonya and a son Roddy who became the second loves of our earthly lives. With the help of the Lord, our First Love, we reared them to believe that Jesus has all of the answers and that serving Him should be our first goal as believers.

Tonya has home-schooled two precious boys through high school (Garrison is now a sophomore and Spencer is in his first year of Bible College), and her husband Alex serves as the comptroller for a firm nearby. Roddy and Amy have two children, Madelyn Joy and Mark, who are a bit younger. They attend Christian school, and Roddy and Amy serve at a Christian college campus in northern Pennsylvania.

In addition to precious family, the love of a wonderful church family and a huge number of friends who have encouraged us along the way in this journey is a wonder to behold. We found that frequent updates of our journey were the way for our friends to have direction as they prayed. When we sat down and wrote the first "Update" of the experience you will come to know, we could not begin to realize how that means of communication would be used. While I am not a social media savvy person, many friends and family are, and we began receiving much encouragement to keep the updates alive. I am a fierce believer in II Corinthians 1 where we are admonished that, through the aid of the Holy Spirit, God will use our difficulties to encourage or teach someone else in the future. And He can do that through any one of us, so long as we are willing vessels.

July 23, 2013, was a day that would be a pivot point in our lives. You will read about that day early in this book. This was the day when I received a partial hip replacement as the result of a fall hundreds of miles from home; it was also the day that would precipitate a cancer diagnosis that came seven months later. The most overwhelming aspect of the story is that, had the "accident" not happened, we would likely not have had the cancer diagnosis soon enough to have had more than a few months of my earthly existence left after its pronouncement! Lung cancer is ferocious in its attack on the body, and often there is very little window of opportunity for treatment. In fact, I was completely asymptomatic, and thus we had no reason to be suspect of such an issue. My goal in writing is that you may know, as we quickly discovered, the blessing of leaning upon the Lord in such a time of trial.

Having been a Christian school English teacher for thirty years, God had instilled in me a love of writing in a passionate sort of way. Writing updates would fan out to our multitude of prayer friends, and it became great therapy. The encouragement of many friends as we posted weekly updates throughout the surgery and treatment period has led me to pen the following pages with a three-fold goal.

First of all, my prayer is that you will come to know (if you are not already so blessed) that catastrophic illness can be a sort of challenge that we can come to endure with grace; until the Lord calls us home, we can be a testimony to both believers and unbelievers. The display of God's grace and power at these times is nearly incomprehensible! Updates became a means of posting where we have been and how the Lord has demonstrated His presence in this previously unmitigated water. He loves us and chooses to use us, and we do not need to understand the why of our circumstances. Deep faith in our Lord and a good and positive attitude are wonderful tools for the journey, and we can truly be victorious!

Secondly, I wish to alleviate some of the uncertainty that comes when we must navigate cancer and cancer treatment. I knew nothing; in fact, I still know very little. I believe, however, that the school of experience might just be an aid to someone else who might face this journey after me. Perhaps you are not the patient, but you are in the role of caregiver. This is for you, too. And if you are simply wondering how to deal with a friend who has cancer, I am writing for you, as well. Each cancer experience is unique, and as you read, you may be saying, "Well, that isn't how I experienced…" That is fine, and the Lord has someone special that He still wishes for you to mentor and encourage. Despite the uniqueness of each journey, there tend to be multiple similarities among cancer patients as well as those with other catastrophic ailments.

Navigating a catastrophic accident or illness away from home also adds a unique challenge, one for which we had never truly prepared. We are encouraged that there may be a thought or suggestion that others may find valuable in a future journey. The Lord provided some wonderful people to guide our direction hundreds of miles from home, and perhaps you or someone you know will profit from what we learned.

Finally, I pray that as you read, God will bless you with a sort of spiritual adventure that will help you to grow. We sometimes flounder for words and actions when we face friends who are fighting this battle. No one plans to get a cancer diagnosis, and at best, the cure rate is an uncertain variable; but we can choose to have victory in the number of days the Lord grants us, and we can survive with grace to enjoy a meaningful existence. Truly, any experience that throws a curve ball into any of our lives is a significant experience when we realize we are the target! In fact, the over-riding principle is the same; God is with us in every stormy cloud, large or small, and He stands ready to comfort and guide. I pray that your heart may be touched to come to know Him or to know more of His presence as you read.

These goals have become a passion that I love to share because of the way the Lord has worked in our lives. The updates that we wrote (and continue to write), the cards and phone calls and countless verbal expressions of encouragement from family and friends, and the Lord Himself through prayer and His Word…all of these have served to bring us strength, and for that we can only say, "To God be the glory!" He has helped us to realize that we need to number our days and see His wisdom so that we can live out this journey called life in the most meaningful way possible.

Remembering that not every challenge of this life is catastrophic is important. And the blessing of such a reminder continues to lead to the path of what we might call smaller or more incidental issues. God desires to give us strength for the moment, no matter its size or complications. That strength, dear friend, can only come as He provides the mercy and peace and love and grace that we need for the journey. May you find joy for your journey and may you learn along the way and may you be blessed as you read!

Part One
A GATHERING STORM

CHAPTER I
NO, I DID NOT BREAK MY HIP!

"This is the day the Lord hath made; we will rejoice and be glad in it."
Psalm 118:24

God works in mysterious ways, His wonders to perform, and the cancer journey that I am about to share is perfect evidence of that fact. One of the most quoted verses in the Bible, Romans 8:28, tells us that ALL things work together for good, and we agree that the verse and its ensuing explanation (verse 29) are true; so often however, we fail in our humanity to embrace the truth that God is always working for our good and His glory. In our minds, in the tough times we may quote that familiar verse, but often our hearts are far from embracing its reality.

In July 2013, a profound stumble on my part led to a broken bone that was the only avenue that would have likely led to the rest of this story. In fact, were it not for a broken hip, I would likely not be able to recount the events of this journey. Despite the pain and the fact that the beginning of our story has nothing apparent to do with lung cancer, God had chosen to teach us, to conform us, and to use us to honor Himself! It would be almost a year before phase two of this God-allowed adventure would reveal an ugly truth!

As you read this chapter, you will likely find yourself wondering why you are reading about a broken hip accident in a book that is about lung cancer. There is no cancer diagnosis or treatment; so far, there is not even a hint of the remote possibility of a lung issue in a woman who never smoked, never worked with asbestos and never played with chickens (the three major markers for causing lung cancer).

Lung cancer does not tend to announce itself publically, especially in the life of a person with no "markers." Rather, this chapter stands to show how the Lord sometimes works through remote circumstances to bring critical reality of a different sort to pass. Truly, it is in this unrequested broken hip saga that the incredible cancer journey begins. Were it not for the hip incident, there likely would be no story such as you will now read!

Having been a teacher for thirty years with all of the "summer benefits" attendant to my position, I remember clearly the excitement and anticipation that had grown as the time drew nearer for our departure from Pennsylvania for our well-planned vacation in Gatlinburg, Tennessee. We would be gone only a week, but it would be a great week!

Having retired from teaching a few years earlier, vacation would not have been so anticipated (Isn't every day vacation day when one retires?) except for the position which I now occupied; the Lord had allowed me to serve in the passion area of my life after "retirement," as director of our local Pregnancy Ministry Center. I would have the honor of working and sharing Christ with teen-aged girls and with women who had found themselves in unplanned pregnancies. I suppose you could say that if there were one down-side to my new ministry, it was that my vacation time had diminished dramatically from my teacher days.

"I am so excited," I remember exclaiming to the executive director of Pregnancy Ministries where I was now employed. As director of the center in my town, I worked hard and loved every minute of the ministry. I admired the volunteers who made our center "happen," and I cared deeply for the gals who came as clients seeking help and most often needing Christ. Our mission statement said that we existed to help women in unplanned pregnancies and that we would offer Christ to them. I found it pure delight to embrace such a ministry.

I had always realized the Lord's hand of direction and blessing on my career and never truly saw teaching in Christian school or involvement in Pregnancy Ministries as work. Rather, they were simply opportunities to serve the Lord and be in places that I absolutely loved. I must pause to tell you how much I loved my husband Roger's willingness for me to forego the pleasure that could have been afforded by my advanced degree in education, had I remained in the public school system. There was no insurance and no retirement and there were multiple grades for which to prepare. Despite the hard work, I enjoyed every day in Christian education, and I had always loved my calling.

Despite all the blessings of PMI, a time of refreshment and relaxation with my precious husband Roger would definitely be appreciated. We had rented a beautiful cabin in Gatlinburg, Tennessee, and the day finally dawned when we could journey the hundreds of miles to our gorgeous week-long retreat. We had stayed in the same cabin years earlier and it had lost none of its charm. Becoming settled and content in this lovely cabin was not a difficult process. Everything was as perfect as we remembered from the earlier trip.

Day three of our vacation, Tuesday, July 23 dawned as an incredible display of the handiwork of our God; we sat in the quaint red rockers and drank our coffee on the front porch of the cabin. The breathtaking views as the scene in front of us changed from heavy cloud to gorgeous Smokey Mountains was a delight to behold. The smoky residue slowly lifted in front of us and every moment, it seemed, was a greater delight than the moment before. The coffee tasted good, the birds sang in chorus, and in our debate about how to spend this day, we had decided to visit Cades Cove.

Touted for its beautiful drive and the opportunity to see log cabins, tiny churches and graveyards that would allow one's mind to wander and wonder about the past, we prepared for the perfect day. We had been through Cades Cove on the earlier trip, as well, but this time, we would stop at every exhibit and drink in the beauty of the mountains and the sweet yet sobering stillness of graveyards of antiquity. The day was good!

At about 3:30 in the afternoon, we approached the last of the log cabins in the Cove. Truly the day had been special and we were exhausted, and Roger made the brilliant suggestion that we forego this last show of antiquity… but I insisted that we finish the day by making the final stop. Because he loved me, we stopped.

At this point, and quite without warning, our vacation took a sudden, unexpected turn as we left the car for the trek to the old log house. Suddenly, I was head over heels and had dropped to the ground with a thud. The concrete stopper that was intended to alert drivers that it was time to stop the car had wrapped its invisible tentacles around me, and down I went! I remember dropping squarely onto my right side, and I hurt.

In fact, I hurt a lot! Pride, however, attempted to save the day. I sat up gingerly, brushed the dust from my clothes and looked around to see if anyone had observed my klutzy behavior. Hurrying around the car, Roger looked down and said, "You broke your hip, didn't you?" If I could have, I would have answered with an equally brilliant remark, but I couldn't. I did try, thinking that perhaps I could wish away what I already believed to be a very real possibility.

"Of course I did not," I replied… only half believing my own declaration. "Just help me get up," I cried. Gingerly he pulled and tugged and we got me on my feet. Actually, we got me on the one foot that wasn't attached to a horribly painful leg. Being close enough to touch our vehicle, I used my arms to pull myself along and get back in the van. Never did the hurt leg or foot touch the ground.

Assuring my dear husband that we could make it back to the cabin and no, we didn't need to stop at the hospital, we began the painful twenty-five mile trip. Trust me, that word painful means painful!

As we wound our way through the curvy mountain byways and back to our temporary home, the pain screamed even louder.

Not sure if it were even possible, I proceeded to "arm walk" along the porch rail to get to the door. Roger brought a ladder-back chair that served as a walker and we managed to get me into the cabin… the end of success as we would know it for this dearly-sought vacation.

Within a few moments I had allowed my foot to touch the floor ever so gently, and the resulting "POP" coming from my hip area yielded an immediately shortened right leg, decorated at the south end by an uncontrollably dangling foot. To say that we were in a bit of trouble would, for sure, be accurate!

And the challenge was merely beginning. We learned that we had no hard-wired phone service because a storm had knocked it out, and we already knew that these mountains were not friendly toward our cell phones. The hospital was forty-five minutes away and I had brilliantly taken myself from the car to the house. We now faced a return trip and I was literally writhing in pain. I did not want to move and Roger was no match for what had likely become dead weight. He hurried to the neighboring cabin and enlisted the help of a dear man and his ten-year-old daughter who were vacationing there.

With this little girl's constant encouragement despite the fear I could see in her eyes, her dad and Roger moved me as gently as was humanly possible and we were on our way down the windy roads to the guard shack at the entrance to this haven we had anticipated loving throughout the week. Alli and Vic were, to our estimation, our first angels that day. We truly stood in need of help and the Lord used their willingness to lend a perfect hand. Though they live hundreds of miles from us in Mississippi, we have come to enjoy their friendship.

There was a second angel when we arrived at the guard shack. Only God could have orchestrated that a retired pastor, Clifford, would be our first line of defense in navigating the trip to the hospital. Roger asked him if he could drive me or if it would be best to get an ambulance. Clifford's reply was that the ambulance was best for multiple reasons, the least of which would be faster attention in the emergency room. In addition, the EMT could administer some medication for pain. That was a comforting thought until I realized that the meds would do no good! After the guard called 911, he came out to see me, and his immediate reaction was to tell me he was praying and his church would also pray. No sweeter assurance could have come at that moment.

The ensuing week became a blur as partial hip replacement was scheduled eighteen hours after the fall. The pain throughout that time was somewhere beyond excruciating, but the Lord was faithful. No surprise there! And Roger was cheerleader-in-chief. "We can do this!" he frequently encouraged… and with His words and the Lord's help, I was able to endure.

Sometimes crises come in various stages, and thus, the next few days would slowly but surely unravel. While the pain in the hip diminished very little, another issue emerged on the fourth day. I became ill. Pain medications have never been friendly to my tummy, and this event would provide no surprises in that department. "Coffee grounds" was the description by my nurse to describe what spewed profusely from my mouth. The diagnosis: internal bleeding, likely from the stomach.

An endoscopy was ordered for the next day, to be preceded by a chest x-ray. When the doctor who would perform this simple procedure arrived for a consult, and actually as he was about to bid his farewells until our date for the endoscopy, he remarked, "By the way, there is something a bit suspicious on your chest x-ray. You should have that checked when you see your doctor in Pennsylvania." He did not seem to be alarmed, so we weren't terribly concerned about this little bit of diagnosis either.

Still in much pain, we (Roger was my constant companion, leaving only to re-pack us and close up the cabin) were released from the hospital the following Sunday evening, and the tedious trip back to Pennsylvania began. With walking and gentle exercise stops every two hours, we made that journey the next day!

Fortunately for you, you have no idea of the beauty Roger was now travelling with. I was disheveled and in much pain, but he stayed by my side despite the sight. And I will never forget the kindness at every Hampton Inn where we stopped for restroom breaks; they so graciously allowed me to use their main lobby facilities which were pristine and ample in size, a blessing since I desperately needed Roger's help at nearly every turn. That is just the way it is for a little while after hip surgery! In case you haven't noticed, you can mark it down: hip surgery is one of those life events that can be initially utterly debilitating!

Were this the end of the story, it wouldn't be much of a story, but now the real adventure began. God had allowed us that unique privilege of a severe bleed that would require a chest x-ray that would likely not have happened were it not for the broken hip! Most often, we tend not to consider chest x-rays as anything other than routine, but there was no order for that picture within the normal protocol for hip surgery.

Today, I breathe a prayer of thanksgiving for the Lord's gracious allowance which enabled the discovery of a tumor which would be diagnosed much later as lung cancer.

LESSONS LEARNED

- ❖ Remember that no matter what the circumstance, God has designed each day especially for you… REJOICE!
- ❖ Never doubt the power of the Lord in situations that may otherwise seem impossible.
- ❖ Have a disaster plan for unplanned catastrophes away from home. For us, because of the extent of my injury, a larger hospital with a specialist in my particular need would have been a good thing… and there was one just a few more miles away.
- ❖ Make some calls or text or establish a care page so that you can enjoy the invaluable support of prayer warriors. We later learned that our prayer team was literally extended around the world!
- ❖ If you don't text and you have no access to email, the old-fashioned phone is a wonderful concoction. We were in close contact with our daughter and son, and nearly everything we shared with them landed on a Facebook page.
- ❖ Every day is a day from the Lord and we can choose to rejoice and be glad! There were some very tough moments, but we never doubted that God was with us, and even an accident can be used by Him.
- ❖ Keep short accounts. Since every day is a gift, we ought never to assume we have tomorrow (or even the next minute) to make amends.

CHAPTER II
IT'S ALL ABOUT PAIN!

"My grace is sufficient..."
11Corinthians 12:9

With God's grace and Roger's patience and the moment-by-moment prayer coverage during our trip home by so many friends, after a journey divided into two days, we pulled into our driveway. Never had home looked so great! Roger got me settled and Tonya and family dropped by for a bit. Roger settled into a routine that he had no idea would last for months that would turn into nearly two years. If a chore needed to be done, due to the incessant pain I was experiencing, he nearly always completed the task. He never complained and he continuously watched for what he could do to ease my burden. He carried a much heavier burden, I believe, as he cared for both of us than my challenge of a recovering hip.

The next few months were not easy. Finding a doctor who would care for me and remove thirty-seven staples was difficult; one office receptionist suggested that we return to Tennessee. She explained ever so kindly that the doctors in that practice did not deal with the problems of other doctors! We finally found one who removed the staples but could find no reason for the pain. We found another orthopedist who looked at the x-ray he had ordered of the partial replacement in Tennessee, and he stated that he, too, could find no problem. I now had two hard copy x-ray pictures from two different doctors near our home and the original Tennessee x-ray; the pictures looked identical, and neither Pennsylvania doctor could find any problem. "Besides," the one doctor quipped, "I wouldn't touch anything or make any repairs for at least a year if I did find an issue." Ouch!

The pain continued to dictate my ability to function. I was accepting an increasing number of the routine challenges of homemaking and cooking and housework, but no task was easy and all of them took two or three times the amount of effort to complete compared to the "before surgery" mode. With the help of Roger, our kids Tonya and Roddy, and my sister Janet, and numerous friends, I was able to concentrate on putting one foot in front of the other (quite literally). And the pain continued.

There was a pivotal phone call from a college friend in Baltimore in September. This call qualified in our thinking as a God-send! As I think of the ways the Lord orchestrated that unknown needs should be met, this call qualifies for that list! Martha, a college friend who now resided in Baltimore, had endured two hip replacements and she said, "Bev, you shouldn't be in this much pain. I wish you would come and see my doctor."

On October 15, I reached Dr. Ebert's office by phone and explained my plight. A kind receptionist apologetically explained that the first available appointment with the doctor was in mid-January. I quickly responded that I would take it, and we waited patiently for the next three months to pass. Martha had sung his praises and had explained that he did little beside his specialties, hips and knees. He would be worth the wait. The receptionist had explained that I would be put on a waiting list, should there be an earlier cancellation. I may receive a call to come earlier. Sadly, no call ever came as we awaited January.

I had ignored the caution from the Tennessee doctor about the chest x-ray because there seemed to be a deluge of problems connected with the hip, and I was in a "one thing at a time" mode due to the discomfort. In honesty, there were times when my mind remembered that caution, but I simply did not have the energy to pursue a clearer diagnosis. To any coward who might be reading this book, such a choice is anything but brilliant. Never wait. If there is a problem, it will likely need treatment and it is highly unlikely to disappear of its own volition! And besides that, who among us does not know that the early bird in any treatment diagnosis is ahead in the "fix it" game.

Saturday, January 18, 2014 was a turning point day in the hip misadventure! As Rog and I waited in the examining room for our appointment with the highly recommended Baltimore hip surgeon who would become my new best friend, I clutched the photocopied x-rays from the two local orthopedists who had been unable to find a problem. The pain in my hip had been constant and severe for several months since the first surgery, and I eagerly anticipated this new miracle-working surgeon whom I would finally meet. Dr. Ebert walked into the room, shook our hands and introduced himself… and he took the x-rays and studied them intently, for what seemed like a brief second.

"Here is the problem," he quipped. "If you look at the ball that was placed in your hip, you will be able to see that it protrudes significantly from your socket." As he pointed to the egregious misfit, sure enough, the problem was so very evident that even our novice eyes could understand. He told us that the new ball from the Tennessee partial hip replacement was significantly too large. And then the words that we longed to hear: "We can fix this with a total hip replacement."

"How soon?" was my only question. Finally the date of March 17 was established for surgery. We left the office with a folder full of instructions, pre-op questionnaires and insurance information. Little did I know, but that appointment was a life-saving one!

And by the way, paying a bit extra for "portable" health insurance becomes a great benefit when accidents and treatments are out of state. For anyone who may leave his state of residence and need health care, this type of insurance could become significant. We were able to move seamlessly from state to state for the necessary treatment, and there were no long delays as medical professionals sought permission for treatment. That included the care in Tennessee, hundreds of miles from home, as well as the selected hip surgeon who was only sixty miles from home but in Maryland instead of our home state of Pennsylvania.

The following business day, Monday, I called my family doc to schedule all of the pre-op exam items that were called for. Rog went with me and as we sat waiting for the doctor to come into our sterile examining room, I knew in my mind that I must mention the "little spot" that had been detected in the

Tennessee chest x-ray. Just in case I had forgotten this little secret, Roger reminded me with a no-nonsense nudging. I would "fess up" for sure this day.

We quickly moved through all of the pre-op steps, and as the doctor was about to leave the room, I said as casually as possible, "By the way, Doctor, I was told in Tennessee that there was a small spot on my lung which should be followed." Looking at me somewhat quizzically (kind of like "Why am I just now hearing about this?"), he wrote an order for a follow-up chest x-ray that same afternoon. Isn't it typical how we can KNOW there is a physical problem and we think we can speak or ignore it away? How many women notice a "small lump" in a breast self-exam and hide it because they are sure that will make it disappear?

When I heard my doctor's voice on the phone a bit later that same afternoon, I knew the news was not good. Typically as for most patients, my doctor had never before called me at home. And now with this first call, he was kind but definitely also in no-nonsense mode. "Tomorrow morning at 8:00, you are scheduled for a CT scan. I will see you by appointment to review the results." Now, it doesn't take rocket science to know that it's not a good thing when a CT scan is ordered for a small spot on the lung.

A couple of days later, when the doctor walked soberly into the examining room for the "report card visit," my first remark was, "This is not good, is it?" I remember glancing at Roger who had the most panicky look I had ever seen on his face.

Hanging his head, the doctor answered quietly, "It is not." My head whirled and my eyes became fairly moist as he explained the need for a biopsy and a PET scan. Incredibly, my hip seemed better than it had been in months, and I was now just two weeks out from the second hip surgery which would fit me with a total hip replacement. Despite that fact, life was looking fairly complicated. What would be next?

As the doctor left the room, I noticed as he compassionately touched Rog on the shoulder. I believe he was as devastated as we were at that moment. How the Lord would unfold the rest of our story full of His power and grace was yet an unknown, and we would quickly learn what it means to "wait on the Lord." A husband's arms become the greatest earthly comfort one can hope for at such a time as this, and I was graced by the comfort of those arms. We had been married for more than forty-five years and we could remember His strength when Roger had suffered a heart attack in 2001; somehow, this event, too, really seemed "big time" major!

As the result of this meeting, we were acutely and suddenly aware that more than likely, we were facing not one, but two major surgeries. At this point we were still in the fog concerning the lung issue, and we had been fast-tracked to a second hip surgery in just a few weeks. The greatest blessing I could mention from an earthly perspective was that, from experience, I knew that once anesthesia sets in, a patient becomes aware of no pain, no matter the surgery. That sounded most reassuring to me!

In the interest of complete disclosure, there were times of major stress within this week. We knew that we would finally be dealing with the "little spot" on the lung and that did create anxiety. As is true with any family where members are close to each other, Roger was impacted in such a painful way. Sleep was difficult and even clearing his mind of what could be ahead was nearly impossible. He and our children and their families were living with the face of death cruelly staring at each of them on my behalf. Oh, how I longed to take their pain, but I could do nothing physically to help them emotionally. I found myself praying on their behalf as I had never before prayed. And I asked the Lord to protect our grandchildren whom I believed had the ability to "pretend" nothing unusual was happening while they were, in fact, deeply vulnerable to doubt and hurt and pain.

Lest anyone would think that fear is to be gloriously abandoned in such a time, please know that we quickly faced the reality that it is perfectly normal to experience fear. We know God tells us to never fear, and I am thinking that He wouldn't have given that advice except that He created us and He knows our every weakness. He knows we will sometimes feel deep fear, and we have His promise that He will always stand ready to help us. And He has been constantly with our family, giving us the blessed feeling of His presence.

When this event really began to move, we would ALL learn even more than we had probably ever dreamed that God could teach us and how to seek His perfect peace and presence moment by moment through this experience. Our major source of anxiety was simply the unknowns that faced us. It was much like the pronouncement of a severe storm when the forecasters had no clue the path that it would actually take. We could not anticipate the future.

The words of a familiar hymn come to my mind: "My Lord knows the way through the wilderness; all I have to do is follow." So often, we glibly sing the words of the great hymns of the faith and we really are not impacted by them. What, exactly, is the "wilderness" in my life or in yours? Quite literally, I had never before been forced to fend my way through such a place! And the hymn uses that preposition "through." A wilderness is a desolate and sometimes difficult place through which we must maneuver. We can't go under it or over it or around it, but rather we must go through it.

The greatest GPS system may lead us accurately through areas heretofore unknown, though it lacks the serenity and faith that come when the Lord is doing the maneuvering. We have occasionally found ourselves lost when we followed our GPS. Emotional or spiritual wilderness does not respond to a GPS system. And fortunately, our family was now embarking on a journey that, although undesired, would be led by the hand of our mighty Lord and Savior. If ever there was peace, it would be in that fact of His care and presence. And we could be fully confident that He would see us through this wilderness journey. His grace would be sufficient in the midst of this increasingly ominous storm.

LESSONS LEARNED

- Life can bring its hurtful moments, but God is always there. He is sufficient!
- He will provide the perfect answer; in our case, the answer would be, in part, an orthopedic specialist from Baltimore, Maryland.
- At least consider the possible merits of PORTABLE health insurance.
- Pray for children and grandchildren, and also determine to be honest with them. They will see through a web of deceit, even if it comes with the best of intentions (to protect them).
- Know that He supernaturally showers us with His love and grace and mercy and peace.
- HIS grace is ALWAYS sufficient!
- Prayer and an open heart and mind have the power to connect us with the Lord's perfect solution in crisis.
- We should never be afraid to face the giants in our lives, even if the process brings tears. After all, God created the tears and He provides the manual for dealing with them successfully.

Part Two
A STORM IN PROGRESS

CHAPTER III
THE CANCER JOURNEY BEGINS!

"My God shall supply all your needs according to His riches in glory."
Philippians 4:19

What an incredible and, thankfully, indisputable promise! God would supply all of our needs, and our family had become very needy people. My prayer continues to be for our family who would walk through this storm with us despite our not knowing its extent. They would be deeply impacted by this storm.

No one ever expects to have the word "cancer" attached to his or her name. Cancer is a horrid disease. The very word strikes fear into anyone's heart, and besides, we had already done our share of cancer journeys. Both my dad and Roger's mom had suffered in unimaginable ways before the ugly illness had strangled their lives from them. For both, death had been slow and so very full of suffering. While Roger's mom suffered in less traditional ways with sporadic pain and utter fatigue, when her death came, it was a traumatic, although brief night as we kept vigil. My dad's cancer was the obvious daily and excruciatingly painful kind, and I remember praying every morning for nearly two months that the Lord would just relieve his suffering and take him home.

We all attempted to maintain an attitude of peace throughout this journey, but the fact is that we lived in a kind of quiet panic and fear that my life would be much shorter than the vapor we had always understood to be true for each of us. We had been living our lives in the Lord's strength, but also with the attitude that life on earth was far from over. Such a diagnosis serves as a reality wake-up call to the truth that we tend not to think about. Life on earth can be unexpectedly brief for any of us! I do pray that the quietude that we generally experienced publicly was an answer to our prayer that Christ would be honored and elevated as we walked this road. And make no mistake; more often than not we experienced peace privately, as well.

Our daughter Tonya was the earthly strength of both of our lives. Having walked the journey of a massive stroke with her then thirty-eight year old husband a few years earlier, she was now one of those vessels that comes forth as gold. Her wisdom and strength often made me feel weak and incapable, and yet she always had the right words and the strong faith that we could draw upon. That she truly was in the palm of His hand was so comforting to us. She became our II Corinthians 1:3-4 God-send because she had already been in the troubled waters of a sudden, severe storm.

Son Roddy was a different kind of strength partner; living three hours away and being enmeshed in a ministry career that claimed inordinate amounts of his time, he became our phone partner. For nearly a year, we heard from him almost every day. I don't recommend our reason for his motivation, but it was surely nice to hear his encouraging voice so frequently. Roddy did share the best of all advice at one point when he assured me, "Mom, it is okay to cry, you know!" And he and his family prayed faithfully.

One of my favorite verses, one that I had, in fact, often prayed through the years, says that this is the day He has made and I will rejoice and be glad in it. "Will" is a modal word, one of choice. Choosing to rejoice and be glad has not always been easy for any of our family through the past couple of years… but it has been possible through His power! Although we would not likely rejoice in the fact of the cancer diagnosis, there are still plenty of reasons to give thanks. It is far better to know that cancer is wreaking its ugly havoc in one's body than to have no idea, thus allowing ever more terrible and adverse consequences.

Countless doctors have reminded us of how blessed I am to have found out that my lung had this little problem. I have often been reminded that without the broken hip, most likely I would never have known of the cancer until it was dramatically too late! Life itself has a far more sacred and precious meaning than it had before the diagnosis. We continue to live as a grateful family, thanking the Lord for His blessings of gifts, talents and circumstances, and the perspective of such an illness has elevated our cognizance of the richness of life to an entirely new level. Truly, HIS reality has set in.

Before the second hip surgery on March 17, 2014, we already had been informed that this was but the first of two major surgeries that would happen quickly! This cancer journey is truly walked with Christ holding our hands; at so many turns, there was a perfect plan that we could have never contrived; only God could have orchestrated what would happen over the next years! So often, personal and intercessory prayers were answered; and sometimes, the prayer wasn't even uttered and God was already working. We are so thankful for our precious Savior Who intervenes on our behalf.

His riches were far beyond our needs and we chose to embrace what we knew to be truth: He would carry us through. We trust that the many miraculous ways that He worked in our behalf will stand out as you read on. We want those who hear of this time in our lives to understand the absolute magnitude of what God might choose to do, quite unexpectedly, when we find ourselves in a catastrophic storm.

One friend called these special events "God moments" and another referred to them as the times when God showed up. Perhaps, it is a narrow interpretation, but while I like those terms, I believe God shows up incessantly, even in the mundane and normal days; that is simply His nature. And when we know Christ and walk through challenging times with Him, every moment is a God moment. He is always so obviously present. I would have been too frozen in fear to move without the inestimable knowledge of His presence!

The result of a meeting with our family doc was that we already knew that quite likely the "little spot on the lung" was malignant. There is an overwhelming sense of inadequacy and helplessness when one hears this diagnosis. So many issues need to be addressed and so many questions need to be answered and doctors need to be trusted and hospitals must be chosen and the list goes on. In the school of life, there is no classroom that can prepare any one of us for this battle. We have often remarked that we cannot imagine how people who lack faith in our wonderful God ever survive such crises!

And did God ever intervene as we were led to the perfect surgeon! We are so blessed to have a wonderful nephew who is a physician at a hospital in a much larger town about an hour from our home. We have always tried to avoid making Dr. Geoff our personal medical encyclopedia at family events or just when the need for a medical answer arrives, but THIS was different! I knew what I needed to do, and without reluctance and with the benefit of my sister's prodding, I called him. He is precious, and I knew he would be my earthly strength and guide with the answers we would be seeking. I realize that having such a resource is a rare and wonderful gift!

"Hey Geoff, its Aunt Bev. I have a bit of a problem here." Nothing beats a direct approach complete with understatement!

"Hi, Aunt Bev…Okay… what's up?"

"Geoff, I was just told that I probably have lung cancer and," as my voice trembled and broke, "I don't know what to do." Without a moment's hesitance, Geoff was kind and gentle and reassuring. After a few moments of conversation, he asked the pivotal question that I had pled with the Lord that he would ask.

"Aunt Bev, do you want me to help you with this?" Oh thank you, Lord, for Geoff's sensitivity.

I've got to be honest. I didn't even pray about my answer to that question! "Oh Geoff, would you? I don't know where to turn."

As you can imagine, I really don't remember much of the ensuing conversation, but I do remember a few details. Geoff explained that he was in a different medical system from the one in our town. For him to become involved I would need to transfer all of my medical information to the system with which he was affiliated. No problem there. My faith in this precious nephew was beyond unwavering and I knew that he would be my greatest advocate, and in fact, he would even be my guide at every turn. He and his dear wife and daughter who lived a stone's throw from the hospital would be so special to Roger and me as we moved forward. Over the next days, we talked to Geoff often. I called him with my questions and he called us with his encouragement. Truly, he was our lifeline to sanity!

Sadly, navigating the process of finding the best doctors sometimes is slow, and it can be daunting! I often wonder if we would have been scheduled for the first appointment with our surgeon so quickly, were it not for our conversations with Geoff. We will never know the answer to this question, but we will be forever grateful for how swiftly the process moved. In addition, the wisdom that Geoff could provide because of his brilliance as a medical doctor will always be remembered. A relatively new term in doctor's offices is the word, navigator. For sure, Geoff was our navigator through this situation that we could barely comprehend. Thank you, Lord, for my sister Jan's insistence that I call her son, and thank you for Geoff's willingness to roll up his sleeves in our behalf!

I must stop here and follow a rabbit trail briefly because it leads to a lesson learned. Soon after Geoff had completed his medical training and was an official doctor, we had a family gathering. Roger's heart attack had been recently enough to still be on our minds, and it wasn't long until we had cornered our personal "expert" to get his advice on Roger's situation. Somehow, I remember getting the message that everybody now considered the good doctor "fair game" as a personal "Dear Abby" for medical questions, and we decided we would not be those kinds of people… and I believe we maintained that stance for years.

Sometimes, however, circumstances in our lives change. In our state of overwhelming emotional chaos, we truly needed someone with whom we could connect, someone whom we could trust and in whose advice we could truly relax. We were blessed to have Geoff, and only the Lord could have ordained his "Would you like for me to…" attitude. God loves us and He knew (no brainer) that we needed someone like Geoff at this point. Geoff's gentle spirit and listening ear through the next couple of years meant so much! We never see him that I don't get a big hug and a genuine "How are you doing, Aunt Bev?" We were also blessed as he and his wife and daughter shared their home and their time with Roger as we were not close to our own home. Only a gracious and loving God could show up with such a God-send as our nephew for this time. And now back to the event.

We had delivered a copy of the CAT scan to the office of the surgeon Geoff recommended. The trip between the two locations (where the scan was performed and the doctor's office) was nearly two hours. The PET scan had been scheduled for the next morning and Geoff told me that we would likely need to get those results to him as soon as possible, so that he could assemble a team and they could make a joint evaluation of my case. We gladly made both journeys, anticipating the best possible care would follow.

At 10:00 P.M. on that Thursday evening, our phone rang and a kindly man introduced himself as a friend of Geoff's and said he would likely be a part of my medical team (he even introduced himself by his first name, helping us to know we had not only gained a great professional, but also a new friend). He was in no rush, and as I remember, the conversation lasted nearly half an hour. We agreed that Roger and I would deliver a copy of the PET scan to his office as quickly as we could the following day.

We would deliver the treasured document on Friday afternoon, but it would now go to a newly selected doctor. As the "team" had evaluated the records that they had already been able to access, they had determined that a pulmonary thoracic surgeon was likely the best person to make the next decision. We had not even been aware of their "behind the scenes" conversations on my behalf. Miraculously, it had been a mere forty-eight hours since my first conversation with Dr. Geoff.

On Friday morning, before we left home for the PET scan, the phone rang. A perky-sounding woman introduced herself and said that she was from Dr. B's office and she understood that it would be good for me to see Dr. B that afternoon. I remember distinctly her next words: "I am calling to help make that happen." Sure enough, at 1:30 on Friday afternoon, we sat in an examining room, clutching the copy of the morning's PET scan and anxiously awaiting this doctor who would be in charge of my treatment. Again, we believe that God surely orchestrated this good doctor's appointments being at Gettysburg rather than York (another hour away) on Fridays, and of course, it was now Friday! We were forty-five minutes closer to home.

Our entrance to the doctor's office had begun with a reality check that neither of us was really prepared to handle. In huge letters above the entrance were two words: CANCER CENTER. If there is anything other than the Lord's grace that can prepare a person to walk through those doors, I surely do not know what it would be! The room was well-appointed and those in charge were well-prepared and friendly… but I do not think either of us could honestly say we were at ease. The sign had been daunting.

Dr. B clearly explained my situation and the options. The team had agreed that whether or not the spot was malignant, due to its size, it needed to be removed. I could take a few months and heal from the hip surgery before lung surgery was scheduled, or the surgery could be scheduled rather soon. As Roger and I looked at each other, no words were necessary. We both knew that if there was even a chance of cancer, the ugly tumor must come out pronto. I relaxed in the fact that I would be spared the biopsy that had been prescribed by the initial surgeon in Maryland.

Lung surgery was scheduled for April 28, a mere month after the second hip replacement. I endured physical therapy for the new hip, and we did everything we knew of to help me prepare for the looming lung surgery. Days flew by and we were in the hospital again before we knew it!

Our son Roddy, daughter Tonya and my sister Janet were gathered to pray and support Roger. And we had already been blessed by a huge support system of church prayer warriors, Pregnancy Ministry friends and a third e-mail list of family and other friends. Roger had set up a means by which we could quickly update those who were so faithfully praying. And Roddy's position at Baptist Bible College in northern Pennsylvania had enabled the web of praying and caring friends to extend even further.

And there was another added blessing. I am sure that I was the typical surgery patient anticipating the unknown. Not surprise-ingly, God had His arms so tightly around me; He and Roger encircled me constantly. He had given me an absolute sense that ultimately, I would be physically healed. I can truly say that I did not concoct this outcome, but God had placed it in the depths of my spirit and soul. With faith and trust firmly planted in Him, I was wheeled to surgery as I quoted my "gurney journey verse," Psalm 18:2. "The Lord is my rock and my fortress…" That is the extent of what I remember having quoted. I slept peacefully (I think), as the doctors worked and countless people prayed.

LESSONS LEARNED

- ❖ God allows no trial without an accompanying solution. In the case of my lung cancer, the solution began immediately with a call to a precious doctor-nephew. God does supply every need
- ❖ There are no insurmountable obstacles when God is in charge.
- ❖ Our God stands ready with encouragement, protection and answers; we just need to follow His leading.
- ❖ We must be ready to admit that we stand in need of the Lord all of the time, and we also need someone "with skin on" sometimes; pride should never stand in the way of our need!
- ❖ Family and friends always stand ready to help even when they don't know how to do so. And they are willing learners. Often, they are eager to hear the sick one articulate specific needs.
- ❖ Be sure to follow up with how the Lord is working after you ask people to pray!! They want to know what is happening.
- ❖ A husband of forty-seven years is, perhaps, the greatest earthly blessing a woman could ever hope to have.
- ❖ Once again, I sing the praises of anesthesia. You have to love that stuff when a scalpel is about to assault your body!

CHAPTER IV
NOT OUR PLANS, BUT HIS!

"But those that wait upon the Lord shall renew their strength; they shall mount up with wings as eagles, they shall run and not be weary, they shall walk and not faint."
Isaiah 40:31

For the record, I believe that the day of surgery is always more difficult on those who are waiting than on the patient! As I slept peacefully (at least, I continue to believe it was a peaceful sleep), my family kept an anxious vigil. Knowing that God has a perfect will is a great comfort; from an earthly perspective, knowing that His will could fast-track one to Heaven is a bit daunting. Make no mistake; I know I am heaven-bound and I look forward to that first glimpse of our wonderful Lord and Savior, but this earthly tunnel-vision life that I lead holds so much anticipation. There are grandchildren to graduate, to marry, to provide us with great-grandchildren; there is a fiftieth anniversary not too far away... you get the picture! I was not the only one in this little family event who had such feelings. I can only imagine the awkward silences, probably tears, reminisces and whatever else would accompany the wait as the Spirit of God hovered with my dear family in the waiting room.

After several hours, Dr. B came out of surgery to assure everyone that all had gone well and I was in recovery. By his estimation, the cancer-- and one-third of my right lung-- were gone. Several lymph nodes had been taken for biopsy, but there was no anticipation that they would yield malignancy. We would wait a week and the results would be official. I had been diagnosed with non-small cell cancer of the lung which was easier to "fix" than some of the other kinds of lung cancer.

During this time of waiting, Dr. Geoff's wife and parents had stopped at the hospital. Roger tells me that there was truly a time of rejoicing in what the Lord had done and Dr. Geoff's father-in-law, a retired pastor, led the little group in a prayer of thanksgiving. These unexpected and very welcome guests had arrived at a perfect time. And there is a lesson in their visit. Effectual fervent prayers of thanksgiving are as appropriate as those of petition. God delights in our thanksgiving and He delights in planning the timing of those friends who will pray and encourage with their visits.

We are all different, but most of us, after an exhausting time in the waiting room, are happy to see a new and friendly face. Never be afraid to visit; if your presence is obviously coming at an inconvenient time, you can always share a hug and a word of encouragement and perhaps even a prayer, and then depart quickly. A couple of cookies or a piece of fruit left in your trail may never hurt, either. After the "Never be afraid..." there is one caution. There are some people who truly do not want anyone to visit. You will generally know who they are because they will be most transparent in telling you so. If they are in your church, they may even have the pastor announce their wishes on Sunday morning. Respect them, don't attempt to change their minds, and stay away. In these cases, a card is definitely an encouragement for them.

We thought that the worst event of the cancer journey, the surgery, had now been accomplished and I could begin the get well journey. Before I knew it, I was settled into a room at the hospital and our visitors were headed back to life at its normal pace; Roger and I rejoiced a lot at the apparent good news. His presence on a bed-type of chair by my side was especially comforting anytime I awoke that night. I am sure that first twenty-four hours yielded a horribly uncomfortable night for him. I know there are some patients who would want the world to leave them alone at this point, but we have always done everything together and I loved Roger's presence and his comforting arms and his words of encouragement. Sadly, in many ways, we were in a re-run of two previous (and recent) hip surgeries. He did spend two nights at Geoff"s home.

The next three days were uneventful. As I lay in the bed, often with my hand in Roger's, we concentrated on the complete healing that we had been assured was ahead. There was no bleeding nor were there any transfusions (as there had been in Tennessee), and I tolerated the pain meds well. We were definitely on the glory road, and that road led to home around noon on Thursday. The trip was just over an hour... a lot easier than the eight hours from Gatlinburg with a new hip... and soon I was settled in and Roger was able to relax a little.

My sister Jan, who has a thriving real estate business that beckons her constantly, had reserved days to come and relieve Roger when we arrived home. She is one of those people with a servant spirit that seems to thrive on the exhaustion that is produced by her serving. I really believe that, when no one needs her, she probably advertises, and thus, she is always on the go. It was fun to have her around even though she discovered that I didn't always clean exactly the way our mom had taught us. Let's just say Jan is always able to find a project that would complicate most of our busy schedules beyond our tolerance.

We continued to anticipate the pathology report which was still a week from delivery. When Dr. B had not called by the following Friday morning, I decided that perhaps I should call him. Roger was running an errand and I was moving quite well, so I perched on the porch swing and made the call. According to the receptionist who took my call, Dr. B was out of the office until Monday. I probably whined a bit at the unexpected delay in results, but I was able to state that I understood and I would wait for a call on Monday. The storm cloud was so very unpredictable at this point.

Within five minutes, however, the phone rang, and I could see that the call was from Dr. B. Immediately, there was the fear (and it was fear, I must confess), that the news was not good despite the original positive prognosis. In that split second of answering the phone, however, I told myself he probably didn't want me to worry through the weekend when, in fact, he had good news. In my heart of hearts, however, I was keenly aware of what could be the worst news. I told myself, however, that he was simply a wonderful, compassionate man who didn't want to make me wait. After all, I had initiated this coming revelation and he had a heart to respond.

Rewind to the bad news option. Gently and kindly, I learned that of the nine or ten lymph nodes that had been removed, the majority presented with some cancer. I didn't cry, but I was in a nearly frozen state of shock. I am thinking that is a typical reaction when such news is given. Dr. B assured me that this was a small and relatively young cancer and he was upbeat that we would have great success when the oncologist determined a treatment plan. I sat quizzically, pondering the attitude that I had always believed to be true for me; I could handle ANYTHING but cancer.

Now, we would embark on the journey of a lifetime where the Lord would show me that although I was correct in that feeling, with Him, all things are possible. While it was true that I could not handle a cancer adventure, a greater truth is that He and I together would be quite a team. I had no problem allowing Him to lead. Isn't that attitude true for all of us believers? With God, the impossible becomes possible. The key is total release of our will to His, but in our humanity, that release is sometimes difficult.

Two thoughts exploded in my mind. How was I going to tell Roger and my family and friends this news? And an oncologist? What exactly would his role be in all of this? Naively, I just figured that Dr. B was competent to get me to the other side of this growing pot hole. I believe that prayer is always the answer to a dilemma, and I knew that it should be the first rather than the last resort, and I found myself praying.

I prayed and thought, and prayed and thought and prayed, and I tried to rehearse the right words for Roger. There is a sort of oxymoron here; what could be the "right words" to say to the earthly love of my life, "I have cancer." I heard his truck and saw it come up the driveway… and there were no words; only tears seemed available in my normally well-equipped verbal tool box. There I sat on the swing, fearfully anticipating the next few moments (actually only seconds) that had the power to alter our lives as we had known them.

A Quick Trip Full of Reflections

Briefly, I reflected on the wonderful history of our relationship. We were raised in Baltimore and attended most of the same schools together. In fact, we were in the first grade class with the same teacher even though nothing in the way of love bloomed at that point. My hair ribbons and his flannel shirt just didn't have much in common. Fast forward to the end of the ninth grade, and a few little sparks began to fly.

Ours was an innocent and sweet relationship blessed by two sets of parents who were always available and eager to spend much time and especially holidays with us. Sundays were always reserved for dinner at my home, with the caveat from Dad that Roger would be going to our Sunday evening church service. That was an agreement written in stone! A summer holiday often yielded a day on the Hannah boat with Roger's parents, and winter holidays stuffed us full as we partook of dinner at both the Hannah and Earnest homes. Our marriage came with the sweet practice of such get-togethers continuing. I might add that a special challenge presented itself the year we enjoyed two dinners at a point when I was very pregnant (Tonya, our oldest child, was born on January 3).

And the rest is history. We had dated throughout high school and college (being two hundred miles apart during our college training). We were engaged at Easter of my senior year; Roger had another year because mononucleosis had thrown him a nasty curve and he had missed a year of school. I lived at home and taught history at a local high school, and he completed his degree and lived at home with his parents. We were married in June when I had completed my first year of teaching and he had carried a diploma across the stage. I was not inclined to put my husband through college and he relented. We waited to marry, as he worked hard and finished college.

We had been blessed to be raised in wonderful Christian homes and we had parents who encouraged us but who never gave us dangerous amounts of "space" in our relationship. We thank them for loving us so much that they desired God's best for us. June 24, 1967, dawned a hot, but beautiful day; we were married at two o'clock that warm afternoon and then we headed for a Williamsburg honeymoon (certain that we would be the happiest company on the Virginia coast).

With our wedding quickly fading into the memories category, we began a wonderful life together. Roger was an engineer and there was little I could do to help him. In fact, I could do nothing to ease his work load because English teachers are not well-equipped to think like engineers. On the other hand, I was a teacher with a desire to be involved in the lives of others, and he quickly embraced that same desire. In my thirty-five years of teaching (most in Christian schools) and four years at Pregnancy Ministries, he was often by my side.

Roger was nearly always with me for the projects I concocted for students or for the events I was required to attend. I could always count on the fact that he would have his sleeves rolled up and he would be ready to help. He was a part of school fundraisers, Bible School, student camping trips, and whatever else the Lord set before us. In fact, I often tease that he could explain the items on a display table whenever we went to churches for Pregnancy Ministries presentations… better than I! I believe he only missed one church visit in the years God granted for us to minister with PMI.

Knowing this bit of our history helps to understand how extremely difficult it was to greet him as he returned home that ominous day! We are a pretty close team. I remember that the sun was shining beautifully, yet we were about to be inundated with cloudy, stormy skies that had assaulted us with a huge storm. What had begun as a pothole was quickly becoming a massive sinkhole. I was already hurting, but I had no doubt that this news would be totally devastating to him, as well. And it was.

Back to the Painful Reality

"Dr. B called and the cancer is in the lymph nodes." Now there's a gentle presentation! It was all that I could choke out and the words tumbled through a mist of tears cascading down my cheeks. And as I remember, I was not the only one with tears. I explained that we would get a call from a cancer center which would dictate our plan for the coming days and weeks. And we wept and we held on to one another and we assured each other that this was going to be okay. Honestly, that was one of only two long, hard cries that swept over me in this event. There were and will continue to be a few tears here and there, but they are so inconsequential. The blessing provided by the peace of God is beyond measure, and it is ever-present.

Now there was one more thing to do. We had to share this news with our children and friends. We debated briefly. My thought was that we would say nothing for a few days until we had seen the oncologist. I am smiling as I write and as I realize that our countenance probably would have alerted the world to our crisis, no matter how hard we tried to disguise our faces. We had been blessed with such a close relationship with our children that a wait of any length before sharing this devastating news would never have worked.

Our decision was made according to Roger's reasoning: we needed to be truthful, completely and painfully truthful with everyone. The first calls were to our children and my sister and Dr. Geoff, and they were tough calls to make. Having heard the original prognosis that the cancer was quite likely excised from my lung, no one was prepared for such a report as we now had to give.

We made the decision to develop an email list which we would use for communication with our prayer friends. Because we are not social media people and I didn't understand the concept of "Care Page," the email means of communication has worked well for us. By the way, I do not understand blogs either, but I have learned enough to wish I had done that. We do know that our updates consistently continue to find their way to several Facebook pages and forwards, and literally hundreds of people continue reading them.

One friend at church explained how he always tacked the updates outside his cubicle at his place of employment, and untold numbers of co-workers would stop to read every new one. Usually I was able to come home from treatment toward the end of every week and write an update; sometimes, by the time I got to the computer, Roger had already completed that task. That was always a great help, and I believe that writing was therapy for both of us.

The Lord truly had given us a vision that these updates could even be a powerhouse of witnessing, a way of sharing Christ with those who had never heard. We have tried to always be faithful in this venture. We continue to sing the praises due to our awesome Lord and Savior, Jesus Christ. One simple chorus, "There's Something About That Name," came often to my mind during this time:

> "Jesus, Jesus, Jesus,
> There's just something about that name.
> Master, Savior, Jesus,
> Let all Heaven and earth proclaim!
> Kings and kingdoms will all pass away,
> But there's something about that name!"

Our overwhelming desire was and continues to be that others will come to know Christ and the power of His resurrection, and that some may learn a special lesson that they need from what we have experienced.

LESSONS LEARNED

- ❖ Do not worry about others seeing your tears; embrace friends at every turn… you need them!
- ❖ Be honest; for the people who love you and care about you, it's only fair.
- ❖ Start writing. Journal and keep a running list of questions for the doc. Also include the good things you might be able to share with him. Oncologists tend not to get much good news!
- ❖ Journal even when you don't feel like doing so.
- ❖ Read your Bible like you have never read it before. Meditate on its words and ask the Lord to direct you to special passages of wisdom and comfort. It's your greatest ally.
- ❖ Know that you can have the greatest faith of your life, and humanly speaking, there still may be some fear.
- ❖ Pray, Pray, and pray some more. Prayer yields the most blessed results you could ever imagine! And even more, it touches the hem of His garment.
- ❖ Always pray continuing to give the entire situation to God's sovereign will.

CHAPTER V
EVERYTHING WE NEEDED TO KNOW WHEN THE TREATMENT JOURNEY BEGAN

"Peace I leave with you, my peace I give unto you…"
John 14:27

Little did we know that we would travel the Information Super Highway in the next little while. We had been concentrating on building a completely open relationship with our kids and relatives and church family and friends, sharing with them and inviting them to pray very specifically for what had become a deep physical and emotional need in our lives. Quite suddenly, the time had come to add the oncologist into the mix. There were days when the absolute feeling of peace seemed to be difficult to find. Yet, we knew that at every turn, the Lord would surely and definitively be with us. We stood on His promise for that, and peace came!

Just in case you should ever have a need to know, even when our children have trusted us implicitly throughout their entire lives, they will tend to doubt that we are giving them the entire truth about this kind of situation. Add a physician into the mix whose name is followed by the term "oncologist" and they become even more wary. Despite the deeply caring and loving relationship we had always had with our kids, Roger and I were acutely aware that our children likely believed we were "protecting" them from the worst imaginable truth every time we issued a new report. We determined to write in the interest of transparency and honesty, and we believe that worked for all.

Our pastor's wife and my long-time friend Linda received calls as soon as possible. In fact, Linda and Jim lived near Gettysburg and sometimes even met us for breakfast after an early morning appointment. We even managed to connect with church friends who often camped in Gettysburg. Every opportunity for fellowship was a blessing, and how special it was to know how much these and other precious ones cared!

One way we found to bring some peace into our children's lives was to sign a document provided by the cancer center that would give them the right to full disclosure about my condition, should they ever desire to check up on us. We do not believe either of the kids ever made such a call to the doctor, but the option provided a confidence safety net, at least. The fact that we continue to call both of them after EVERY appointment, no matter how simple the appointment seemed, probably helped, as well. In fact, those calls are always initiated before we even leave the cancer center parking lot.

Moving Toward Treatment

Two things figure heavily into this period of moving forward. First, we were suddenly aware that frequent trips to the Cancer Center would become necessary. As the journey began, we were not aware that there would be about seventy trips, in the first year alone, to various doctors, blood tests and scans. Since the Gettysburg Cancer Center is about twenty-five miles from our home, those were long trips, especially when they occurred, at the least, every Monday through Friday for seven weeks. Some days, there were two trips separated by several hours and we did the complete exercise two times! There were also multiple trips to Baltimore and to physical therapy in the seventy number. Watching Roger as he drove most of these missions brought so much sadness to my spirit; I felt that there was little I could do to lift the burden, and yes, even the fear that he carried.

Even now, the least we go to Gettysburg is twice a month, once for the oncologist and once for the port to be flushed. Do not do the math; the mileage figure was staggering when we considered that none of these trips, by design, even had any fun connected to it except as we invented fun. Such journeys, compounded by their purpose, tend to bring sheer exhaustion with them. These facts sometimes seemed to nearly rob us of energy and joy.

The second thief of our peace was the fact that we were about to trust my very future to a man whom we had never met, a doctor who would deal with a situation we never dreamed would ever be on our radar. Let's be clear; our precious Lord and Savior was always in control, and He would always be the Pilot, but suddenly there was a person, the oncologist, about whom we knew nothing, and he would be our earthly in-charge man! What a blessing to embrace the Lord's design and equipping of our doctors as well as for us and our situation! In fact, the Lord had given us what I would perceive as an unusual peace to trust whatever the medical staff advised. Perhaps that was because we knew that those individuals were also in the Lord's hands, and He never fails.

I had begun to pray for this initial oncologist's appointment as soon as we knew it was coming. Of course, we both prayed that my situation would not be as serious as was possible. And yes, we even prayed that when this man looked at the reports and did his assigned share of poking and prodding, he would find nothing. I particularly prayed for this new man in my life. Tonya, Roddy and Roger will all tell you that, as "sweet" as I may try to be, my body language speaks far louder than anything I might say when I am stressed and distressed. The drift of what I am not saying, my kids assure me, comes through quite clearly! Perhaps it would be a challenge for me to connect with this stranger, and that was cause for concern. I am thinking it would not be a good idea to have a bad relationship with any doctor, let alone one of such importance.

Realizing that my body language could turn the heart of this professional if he sensed animosity on my part, I began especially to pray for the needs that I perceived the doctor might have. Now, I knew the best prayer would have been to ask the Lord to guard my heart, but it seemed like it would be so much easier if He just took care of the doctor. After all, if he was kind and I "connected" with him, my body language wouldn't be in question!! I would have to admit that some of my prayers were a bit on the lame side, attempting to fix the doctor whom I had not yet met, when I was the one who quite likely was in need of a repair job for my attitude.

May 15 was the appointed date to meet with Dr. R initially, and so we made the journey of forty-five minutes to his office in Gettysburg. I remember there was much quietude, as neither of us could even guess what would transpire in the next hour.

Walking into the building that housed many medical offices and identifying the Cancer Center was immediately easy. The letters that named our destination, Cancer Center, once again seemed to me to be eighteen feet tall! I am not sure we ever truly became accustomed to that title. In fact, we were returning to the same location as where we had initially met the surgeon a month earlier.

"Surreal" is probably the best word to describe how we both were feeling as the automatic doors sensed our presence and swept open. God, in His compassion, had given us a peace that even carried into this meeting. It is possible to have peace despite the sobering effect of certain events. Although we were quiet as we waited, we were not fearful, and I believe that God had chosen to help us to believe everything would go well.

At the receptionist's desk, we were greeted by the first of a myriad of friendly faces whom we would come to call friends; we checked in and then found seats where we could "relax" until our names were called. Scanning the room, I realized that we were among a host of very ill people; many were gaunt and several women sported caps of varying styles. No secret here; I knew they were protecting heads that had become suddenly bald from the dastardly work of chemotherapy. Deep in my heart (actually, right on the surface) my overwhelming concern about my own hair became my elephant in the room. How would I handle baldness? Vanity of vanities, it now seems humorous that of all the tenable issues, this would be the greatest one to plague my mind! I want to share more about this issue later.

Most people were accompanied by a friend or relative, and I noticed that in most cases these guests travelled with the patients when a nurse called the patient's name. It would not be long until I learned that those accompanying guests who did not proceed to the examining rooms were usually awaiting patients who had come for radiation rather than chemotherapy. No company is allowed in the radiology area; even the radiology techs step out of the room before the machine begins its zapping process.

Some people spent their time in chemotherapy alone, but most had company they had brought with them. We quickly learned, to our surprise, that chemotherapy varies not only in formula but also in protocol of treatment. Some receive daily treatment while others have treatments spaced by days or even weeks; some are in the chair for moments, while others spend all day!

As I wandered through the myriad of observations of this new environment, rather quickly, my name was called and Roger and I were ushered into a small examining room. A kindly woman swept into our presence and introduced herself as our nurse navigator. At the time, I didn't know what her title meant, but we quickly realized she would be the eyes and ears and even the scribe for anything we missed in conversation with the doctor. She did the preliminaries that nurses usually do and then explained that we should relax and just listen when the doctor arrived. She would take thorough notes and give us a complete copy before we left.

The Nurse Navigator assured us that we would be inundated with information, and that was a normal part of the process. Not to fear, we could call her anytime with any concerns that came into our minds. And our children could call her or the doctor as well, since we had given permission for the doctor to speak openly with them.

Even though we were feeling as though things were happening too quickly, we were granted little time to adjust to this sterile environment before the doctor appeared. We were properly introduced by the nurse navigator, and after squirting his hands with the antibacterial cleaner that is located at every turn in this place, Dr. R shook our hands and the interview began. My hands remained a bit damp from his antibacterial treatment, but they soon dried and I could focus on him. Realizing the need for cleanliness and a germ-as-free-as-possible environment, we adjusted to many handshakes that were accompanied by slightly damp hands.

Dr. R is tall and blonde and young! My first reaction was to doubt his competence. After all, he was very young (from my perspective)! We were both quickly impressed, however, with his expertise and concern for us. Actually, the interview reminded me a bit more of a dissertation than a time to ask questions; most of those had already been answered by the nurse. And Dr. R. had so many things he really needed to communicate to us. Rather matter-of-factly, he explained the type of lung cancer that we were dealing with, and he reaffirmed that it was the "good" kind, non-small cell. He reaffirmed the surgeon's feeling that the tumor was clearly defined and had been caught early, but he also made clear the fact that lung cancer is difficult to address and there could, for sure, be no promises of cure. Of course, that is true of many cancers, but lung cancer is somewhere in the very difficult category. Undaunted, we listened to what seemed, at the time, like it could well be a death sentence. We simply focused upon remembering that we knew the Great Physician, and whatever He deemed best for me would put me in a winning situation.

It was now mid-May and we were told that treatment would begin in a couple of weeks. After cancer surgery and before treatment, ideally, the body needs some time to heal. In the time between, I would have day surgery for a port to be implanted before chemo began, and there would be a day of measuring and lining my body up for radiation. I couldn't even anticipate what these processes actually would entail.

"Any questions for me?" the doctor patiently inquired as we were likely staring deep into space and attempting to comprehend all that had been explained to us. He had spent nearly an hour with us at this point. I had noticed that the nurse wrote intently and had filled several pages of a legal pad. I would be forever grateful for the opportunity to read her thorough notes in the quiet of our home that evening (and several more times in the next few days). In her notes, she seemed to have a way of making everything practical and understandable.

Questions? Of course I had the same question asked by nearly every woman facing chemotherapy. Never mind about ports and radiation. "Will I lose my hair?" I asked. Now, that surely isn't the most profound question that I could think of, but I am a woman. That was important! I had no clue as to how I would prepare myself if, in fact, baldness were an eventuality. I want to share a journal entry from that day so that you might understand more fully.

"Hair loss… What a minor issue to be wreaking havoc in my mind. Lord, please help me to accept all the little inconveniences that are a natural part of this journey. But just in case you need to hear me say it, I know you can get me through this with no hair loss and I would thank you so much if you choose to do that."

Quite matter-of-factly, Dr. R announced, "You WILL lose your hair in about two to three weeks." Whoa! His answer seemed non-negotiable. It seemed that my particular chemo formula contained the dastardly drug that would nearly guarantee hair loss. I will share a bit more about the hair crisis later.

We asked some other questions, the appointment for the port was made and the date of the first treatment was set. Just as we had already been told, radiation would happen five days a week for seven weeks. Chemotherapy would be administered once every week during the same period. Another PET scan would happen several weeks after chemo ended… and we walked soberly out the door, unfamiliar information flooding our minds.

I remember many nurses speaking to us and smiling in such comforting ways as we left the center that day. We had tried to smile back, but I doubt the success of our effort! We stopped in the very public hall outside of the center and hugged a big and comforting hug. My precious Roger was hurting; sometimes I think his emotional hurt was far greater than my physical weakness.

We would experience spiritual growth through the next few weeks that would be far greater than what we could comprehend at this point. This storm had truly increased as its strong winds blew ceaselessly, making sweeping changes in the landscape of our lives. What we knew beyond the strength the Lord would provide was that quite suddenly, life had become tough... and it had happened so quickly... and we hurt.

LESSONS LEARNED

- BELIEVE He can and will bring peace!
- Expect to be overwhelmed by the magnitude of what is happening.
- Expect the peace that only the Lord can bring to calm the spirit and the soul.
- Have a designated place to write down all the questions that come to mind (no matter how ridiculous they may seem) and take that list to every appointment…with a pen for jotting down answers.
- REPEAT answers to the doctor to be sure you have understood correctly.
- Never fail to ask a question; they are only silly if we do not ask them, and every question deserves an answer! I had learned that fact in my high school teaching days as I encouraged students to ask questions. But I had never expected to need the practice in my own life!
- Take someone with you to every appointment, someone you love and trust. This person will be vital to your strength throughout the journey. It's probably no surprise that Roger was my special person, although occasionally Tonya or a friend came along. I did not hesitate to invite these ladies to join me for doctor conferences.
- Remember that the Lord was not surprised by this journey; He has been present at every turn, and He already knows the end.
- Remember that no place is better than the safety of the arms of Jesus!

CHAPTER VI
ONE MORE HURDLE BEFORE TREATMENT?

"Fear not for I am with you…"
Isaiah 41:10

Smiling, I am focusing on the number "one" in this chapter title. One more hurdle before surgery… what could that be? In fact, there were at least three hurdles. The first was the most tangible; the other two were deeply spiritual and emotional. First of all, a port would need to be placed in my body. There were only two things I didn't know about a port. I didn't know what one was, and I didn't know where in the body it would go. The second issue was being measured and marked for the radiation treatments, and the third was just the overwhelming sense of having no control over my body or my life.

A great lesson for me has been to remember that I am human, created with a full range of emotions: and just like every other person, saved or unsaved, believer in Christ or not, sometimes those emotions go a bit (or a huge bunch) haywire. Most of my friends and my family will tell you that I tend to place hard demands upon my own performance. Though not terribly competitive (My family is probably laughing at this statement), I have never learned how to "fail" with grace. There is a desire for doing things right the first time, and I am often driven; that desire can be difficult for me to surrender. Thank you Lord for Your love and gentle concern at those nasty times! Thank you for Your faithfulness in always bringing me back. Thank you that you know all about ports and radiation and my desire to control the situation.

The First Hurdle: The PowerPort.

According to a free little booklet that was presented by the nurse navigator for my reading pleasure, I offer you the following definition. "A PowerPort offers the unique ability to provide access to power-injected Contrast-Enhanced Computer Tomography scans." Did you get that? Had it not been for the experiential training that was fast to come, I still wouldn't understand it, but I am now thankful for the port! The PowerPort is placed completely under the skin (For me, it was in the chest area). It is accessed, with luck or more accurately with God's help, only once per visit, and then all other needle sticks piggyback into that one line. The line attached to the port goes into one of the large veins that delivers blood to the aorta. Although implanting the port is a brief process, it is completed under anesthesia and the process does carry some risk.

If as you read, your head is now swimming, join me in the utter confusion that we initially experienced. We read and re-read and re-read… and Roger with his engineering mind made sense of the whole idea of a port; I did not. Now that treatment is completely behind us, I can go for days and not even think about this uninvited guest living within my chest. I had chosen to assume that the port would be removed as soon as chemotherapy ended (it often is), but Dr. R chose to keep it in place as a kind of "just in case" provision. Should there be a need for infusion again, already having the port would make the process much easier. I must admit that having it removed had more of an appeal before I learned that, unlike the "installation" surgery, I would NOT be asleep when the port was removed!

I had this lovely brochure that explained everything I never dreamed of needing to know about ports. In addition and probably of greater help, the nurse navigator had carefully explained that, with chemotherapy, a port is the most logical way to ease the pain from countless needle sticks at each appointment. Without the port, there would be at least four sticks each week; one would draw blood to be sure of a healthy blood count before we began chemo, the second would administer anti-nausea medication, the third would allow the chemo to flow into my body, and a final one would flush the port at the end of the procedure. In fact, she told us that we would be in a much safer zone with the port than without it, and abhorring needles as I do made the idea more attractive.

While I could clearly remember that Dr. R had cautioned me of the need for a port to be placed in my chest, I remember that I had not the foggiest idea about the process. When he asked me if I would like to have a particular surgeon operate to place the port, I was at a loss. I knew no surgeons except the one who had done the lung surgery, and as it turned out, he was not the kind of surgeon to do this particular procedure. On top of that, I had never dreamed that this procedure would even be considered as surgery! I really have no idea what I thought it would be, but surely it would not be another surgery, even of the simple "day" or "out-patient" type.

Dr. R suggested a surgical team at the nearby hospital, and an appointment was made for later that week. I would meet the surgeon just prior to the "minor" surgery with all its attendant possible complications. This fact added stress in the protocol since relationships are so important and I really felt I needed to have some sort of heart-to-heart with this doctor before surgery day! As with all surgery, I was forced to sign away my life and all of the "what ifs" that could go wrong during the procedure.

Despite my uneasiness, the Lord had this event planned in a very special way just as he had done with all of the other details surrounding this journey. On May 20, we entered the Day Surgery section of the hospital, and we were checked in to the surgery schedule and taken to a preparation room. A very kind nurse was assigned to my case and she rarely left my side. In fact, when I told her I knew the Lord, she brightened and told me that we were sisters. Thank you, Lord, for a nurse who was sensitive to my need for her to pray… twice. I am so sad that I cannot remember this dear woman's name.

If you have ever had surgery, you know the routine. Arrival at the hospital is required, according to the protocol of the hospital, one to two hours before the scheduled surgery. Roger tells me that I am clock-obsessed, but I do know that we waited at least an hour and fifteen minutes after the assigned surgery time. That's a long wait on an uncomfortable stretcher!

In fact, Roger is right and I am a clock watcher. The habit probably comes from years of teaching when the hands on the clock meant something. When the bell rang, everyone moved to the next class, and there was no room for a slowing of the process. In hospital scheduling, bells do not carry the same significance. They must often be ignored because of well thought out triage decisions or complications in the OR. I understand the principle of gratitude that connects with the fact that mine was a minor surgery, and doctors are making the wisest possible decisions based on patient needs. Nevertheless, the wait was a bit difficult on my patience barometer.

During the wait and after her first prayer for me, the iddy-biddy nurse had returned to our holding room to explain that she would move to her next assignment and I would be cared for by a new nurse as I was wheeled to surgery. I suppose I showed some disappointment that she would be leaving me; I felt I had a trustworthy new friend whose prayers would continue when "the lights went out."

And God worked. When it was time for me to be moved to surgery, my nurse friend reappeared to tell me things had changed and she would be with me throughout the entire procedure. Just before surgery, she asked if I would like for her to pray a second time and I was blessed by her beautiful words. What a wonderful way to fall asleep! I am so thankful for her perceptive note of my desire for her to stay with me!

I have always maintained that once I have gone to sleep before surgery, the doctors are in charge and should do whatever is necessary to correct my problem. At that point, I don't complain (mostly because I can't, probably). After this dear nurse had prayed, I went to sleep repeating my gurney journey verse from previous surgeries, Psalm 18:2. "The Lord is my rock, and my fortress, and my deliverer; my God, my strength in whom I will trust; my buckler, and the horn of my salvation, and my high tower." I am usually soundly asleep before I reach "my fortress"! When I awoke some time later, the dastardly, yet life-easing deed had been accomplished. I woke up rather quickly and we were soon headed home. And I now truly understood the phrase, "I have a lump in my chest."

The truth was that the placement of the port was a major reality check. The fact that something foreign to me was going to be placed in my chest and that it would likely remain there for about a year… that fact drove home so clearly that I was truly ill and the situation was unquestionably serious. My usual Pollyanna attitude was struggling to stay active. The reality of cancer was really striking a hard blow, not only on my body but on my mind and emotions, as well. And in a different way, cancer was sinking its venomous fangs into the lives of my family too.

The bottom line was that the first major problem had been conquered and we were ready to move forward. We simply trusted that the Lord would continue to love and keep us through this challenge. And we prayed that we would never disappoint Him. After all, He had shown Himself so faithful thus far, and we knew we could trust Him to the end. We just didn't know what was between this point and whatever the "end" would be!

The Second Hurdle: Measurements for Radiation.

Measuring was truly a physical process, but once again, mentally and emotionally there was such a profound sense of the depth of illness and the significant role of all of these medical caregivers on that measurement day! Anyone who has ever had surgery understands the brutal truth that modesty is often put on a shelf. It has to be that way, but I found that truth extremely difficult to accept on measurement day. No one can really prepare a cancer patient for this day, even when the patient is blessed with incredibly wonderful technicians as I was.

On an earlier tour of the Cancer Center, I had been shown a room that was very large and sterile, and stark in contents. In the middle of the room was a large radiation tube with a treatment table. Today, dressed in a gorgeous designer gown provided by the center, I now lay on the table in utter quiet as two technicians scurried around, preparing for what needed to be done next. My body would be scrupulously measured and positioned and marked for the "real deal" of radiation treatments which would commence in another week.

As I think of the radiation procedure and the absolute accuracy that it requires, I am amazed at the brilliance of these technicians. I had taught high school English for most of the past thirty years, and I stand to tell you that I could never hope to do what these ladies could accomplish! They were brilliant. They were compassionate and kind and they tried to give me a sense of ease, but they were also focused and obviously serious about their task. As I lay still and they moved my body to exactly the position they knew they needed, I remained silent. I feared that even a word I might utter could skew their measurements. That was a tough task for me, because my typical approach to an ominous event has been to say silly things and try to get everyone to laugh. There could be no laughter this day. When the techs had my body in what they knew to be a perfect position, they explained the next part of the process.

The tattooing process was next on the agenda. The purpose of the tattoos would be to guide the team as they lined me up for radiation every Monday through Friday for the ensuing seven weeks once we began the process. In case no one has ever told you before, let me assure you that tattooing hurts. The procedure is brief, but it stings a lot. There were only two tiny dots, but my body really wanted to stiffen when they did the second one; being a coward caused me to dread a second sting in the worst sort of way. There was great surprise however, as I believe I was expecting Mickey Mouse or Donald Duck to appear, and, in fact, there were only two tiny dots.

Relax if you face this process; my reaction to perceived pain has always been more dramatic than is likely necessary! This process concluded the measuring for the coming radiation assault on my body. I did not know till later that a pillow that identified with my head had been created and would be used to help position me each time I went for treatment.

When I returned to my sweet and ever so patient husband, I was officially ready for the coming journey. I believe he had been in his chair in the waiting room for about two hours on this day. The pain and concern etched in his face was once again brutally evident.

The Third Hurdle: Relinquishing Control.

The third pre-treatment hurdle actually had two prongs, and both would allow for a peaceful transition into treatment itself. I felt that I needed a plan for passing the time in radiation. My "make the moments count" mindset needed to find a way to make this time profitable beyond the physical purpose. And

Roger and I agreed that we needed a plan for survival for the days marching up to treatment. Remember, we had completely placed our faith in Jesus Christ… but I still felt the need to carefully construct a "plan."

First was the issue of profitable time management on the radiation table. Two blessings from my past would help here. Having taught in Christian schools, every year had provided me with the privilege to teach a Bible class. In addition to learning the stories and principles and doctrines of the Bible, my students were required to memorize Scripture every week. Grading their weekly quizzes had been not only a natural but also an easy way for me to memorize a lot of Scripture. I had loved teaching Bible to my teens, but I never realized this particular way the Lord would use Bible memorization from those classes in my own life.

I believe I only taught four different aspects of the Bible curriculum in those thirty years, but gratefully, I thanked the Lord for all of those verses He had helped me to hide in my heart. I had always felt the need to memorize the passages I was requiring of my classes, and it is so true that hiding God's Word in our hearts becomes a wonderful bank of deposit, not only daily, but also for emergency needs. The second blessing was that I had always loved to sing the great hymns of the church and I had memorized lots of them.

Knowing that I could not afford to dwell on what was actually happening during radiation treatments, the above factors worked together to bring satisfaction and peace on this issue. I determined on the forty-five minute drive to the center each day what the day's plan would be. Sometimes, I lay quoting verses; sometimes I sang hymns in my mind and heart. It was not possible to sing aloud, as even minimal movement would thwart the procedure. Still other times, I prayed.

If the day's plan was to pray, I knew when I entered the radiation room what or whom the day's specific prayers would entail. Sometimes I prayed for the medical staff, and at other times I prayed for friends, recent prayer chain requests, everybody I could think of in our church, our family (immediate and extended), the needs of our country, the pastoral staff at our church, cancer patients across our country (even though I didn't know who they were, God knew)… and there was so much more. The list was extensive, and of course, no matter how I chose to worship the Lord in this time, I was always silent and still during the process, fearful that I might move in the tiniest way and get zapped in the wrong spot!

You may ask how that plan helped someone so bent on having control to relinquish that control over the entire situation. The answer is simple. We know that as soon as we put our focus on another person, need or situation, we lessen the focus on ourselves… and we could easily have dwelt upon this circumstance. However, when we are focused on the Lord, all of the less significant mind bogglers dissipate! Try it sometime. It really works. Quickly I realized that I was not so overwhelmed and I actually looked forward to these brief quiet times as I focused on the Lord and on others.

I had come to love and respect and trust the dear ladies who were in charge of this aspect of my treatment and God gave me peace. I should tell the truth: my "plan" was surely not mine at all. It was a plan given to me for my good by the Holy Spirit!

Isn't it a great blessing to realize the many ways that God, through His Holy Spirit, is at work in our lives?

Moving Toward Day One

Now we had done everything required to be qualified for the first day of treatment. The final issue in this phase of our little storm had little to do with treatment and lots to do with our peace of mind. How would we pass those last few days waiting for the coming cancer treatment event? My precious Roger determined that we should enjoy a weekend away immediately before the Tuesday that initiated treatment (Monday was Memorial Day and the center was closed). We found a lovely restored revolutionary era cabin two hours from home in Lancaster, Pennsylvania, and we rented it for two days.

Again, God in His faithfulness did cause us to enjoy the time. I remember no tears or "what if's" or even fear. I would not have thought that could be possible, but with Him, all things are possible! I believe we neither thought nor talked of the impending future much in those precious forty-eight hours. We just enjoyed the time together. I must say again at this point, the blessing of a Godly husband whose arms seem to be able to remove all fear… that blessing is beyond reckoning.

The story of our journey is filled with special "God moments," and one occurred during our little vacation. The woman who rented the cabin to us lived up a hill from where we were staying, and we had instructions to come to her home to pay our bill. The home was beautiful, the setting bucolic. And the doorbell rang with a resounding voice. As she greeted us on her porch, we shared the value of these two particular days with her, and she shared her career which was, in part, being an oncology nurse! I still smile that the Lord had even inserted this amazing orchestration into our symphony. She asked if she could pray for us, and standing quietly, we listened to her pray for areas of our future that hadn't even occurred to us. She had been in the arena and in the battle for hundreds of cancer patients in the past, and she understood completely what we still could not yet comprehend. As she prayed, God was again bringing to our attention some facts that we had not already learned concerning the coming treatment. Only God could have orchestrated such a beautiful song!

On Sunday, we came home from our wonderful retreat and our hearts and minds and bodies were as ready as they could be for the coming week. By the way, there had been no television and no internet in that little cabin retreat; we had the privilege to be reminded of how that absence of modern devices can quiet the heart! Thank you Lord for YOUR rest!

LESSONS LEARNED

- ❖ It is okay to feel apprehension in a strange and apparently threatening situation as long as we know to keep a strong faith in the power of our God.
- ❖ The radiation process is brief but nevertheless lonely, but we never need to be alone; God is always with us.
- ❖ In the case of enduring radiation treatment, a bit of creativity can be a great help. Finding ways to consistently dwell on the Lord will carry one far in the journey. I often wonder how many people spend these moments in the radiation tube staring at the cold, hard surface; I wonder how many are filled with deep fear as they face these moments.
- ❖ Learning to trust the caregivers and medical staff that the Lord has placed on the path is hugely important.
- ❖ II Timothy tells us that God has not given us a spirit of fear and that is true; it does not mean that there won't be fear, and He knew that so He directed us to "Fear not." He is always with us! And He desires to settle the fear and bring peace if we choose to allow Him to do so.

CHAPTER VII
TREATMENT BEGINS!

"The Lord lift up His countenance upon thee
And give thee peace."
Numbers 6:26

Realizing that we were in the battle of our lives with the ominous diagnosis of cancer was, at best, an undesired realization; we began immediately asking the Lord for an extra measure of His grace. We knew beyond any shadow of a doubt that He would be our ever-present source of encouragement and enabling, and there could be no question but that He was the Peace-Giver for this as well as every other situation we would face. Isn't it strange how we take the presence of peace in our lives for granted... and when we need a bigger dose, we quickly find ourselves prostrate before Him? We truly braced for the unknown, knowing that God was already there!

By far, the greatest single event to seem as an ominous dark storm cloud on the horizon was the first day of chemo and radiation. This event would have caused us to cower (as if that would have been protection from the storm) were it not for our faith in the Lord, our ever-present help in time of trouble. His ways are not only perfect, but the strength He gives is perfectly timed and beyond comprehension!

May 27: I checked and re-checked the calendar on the May 27th block (and even on May 26th) to be sure that I had my schedule correctly remembered. I didn't realize at the time that this procedure of holding my brain accountable for calendar accuracy would become a significant challenge over the next few weeks. While I was accurate in anticipating the first day and treatment was, in fact, to begin on this day, we would quickly learn that my memory would take some kind of a hit in this treatment process. In fact, for several months, I messed things up so badly on the kitchen calendar that I was reduced to printing a blank calendar page, cutting it to fit the old calendar page, and taping it to cover the old page. Then I could redo my original page in correct and readable form. A couple of months that first year of crisis, I had two or more revisions. By the way, this form of a calendar "cheat" works in a myriad of messy calendar situations! One thing was for certain for me; I did NOT want to miss my treatment appointments ever, if possible.

My fear of missed appointments, whether they be for cancer treatments or for other reasons, was not really necessary. You see, this giant of a husband of mine is always on top of everything. Although his engineering mindset sometimes frustrated my more right-brained mind, he is truly indispensable, always directly behind or beside me to cover my tracks or to keep me on track! I reiterate that I absolutely had many wonderful family members (who can never escape being in the midst of this trial) and friends throughout this journey, but "husband" was the earthly strength of my life. I do not remember the first time that I heard him pray that I would be healed, but that has continued to be a consistent, daily prayer.

What a blessing for a spouse to be gifted by the expectation that the Lord is hearing such a petition!

A good place to begin this part of the story is with my journal. Therefore, the following remarks come from the lines left for my observations in my now favorite devotional book, *Experiencing God Day by Day* by the Blackaby's:

"First day of chemo and radiation today. A difficult night last night… little rest. Gave a whole new meaning to the precious promise, 'Joy comes in the morning.' As we arrived at the center after a rather sober forty-five minute journey, once again the words CANCER CENTER seemed enormous… maybe twenty feet tall this time!"

"The treatment center is bright and clean and the nurses are so sweet. I was especially happy to see the radiology techs with whom I had already had so much experience. Radiology went quickly. Having chosen to spend this radiation table time counting blessings, I wasn't even aware the treatment had actually begun when the tech came to tell me the day's goal had been met!"

"I think in many ways this is more difficult for my precious Roger than it is for me. I love him so much and couldn't do this without his strong and gentle support. I wish there were a way for me to give to him as he gives to me. I feel kind of like a moocher right now as I even recount what a blessing he is. One thing we have learned together is that the natural fear of the unknown is a special invitation from God for us to rest together in Him."

"Dr. Y {the radiologist} is on vacation this week. I guess that is okay. He needs some time with his family, but I did think he would be there to guide me through the first day. A precious retired radiology doctor was serving in my doctor's stead and he was amazing and insightful. He asked if I was fearful, and of course I told him that I was not. He began to gently help me focus on the beautiful verses in God's Word that instruct us not to worry, to remember the birds of the air and the lilies of the field… and he urged me to think positively, taking no thought of yesterday or tomorrow. A special blessing from the Lord!"

Immediately after the first radiation treatment, we were ushered into the room where we would spend much time over the next seven weeks. Once a week, we would come to this place where the routine would always be the same and the chemotherapy would ultimately slowly ooze into my body. No one had actually walked us through the chemo process, and so we were probably both a bit wide-eyed curious.

A side note: If anyone ever thinks that chemo would be better if no one accompanied the patient to treatment, they would generally be dead wrong. If ever I needed a friend, it was at this time. Several precious friends, our daughter and my sister had volunteered to relieve Roger and make this journey with me. In fact, my friend Linda drove an hour from her home (passing the Cancer Center), she picked me up and drove back to the Center, she waited for treatment to end, took me back home and then turned around and drove back to her home.

Sometimes it was good for Roger to have a break. No one was surprised, however, at the times when he cancelled a scheduled driver because he simply desired to be by my side. And while I loved all of those who stood in line to help, I must confess that I loved his presence, probably in a little bit of a special way. In fact, I don't believe he missed but one chemo treatment... the day the needle had decided to not find its port entry.

The nurse assigned to my chair was very kind and pleasant. She was gifted to put me at ease and be an encourager. She answered all of our questions (mostly Roger's) and the adventure began. First of all, the port was accessed and blood was drawn. Then there was a down time as we waited for lab results to be processed; they would affirm that my body, and particularly my white blood count, were in the acceptable parameters for chemo.

Although poor results never came my way, I often saw patients get "unhooked" from the chemo quickly. That happened generally because the white count was too low. We all understood that event to push out the ending date of this arduous process by another week, at least. For some patients, it would be several weeks (or in a few situations, never) before the counts were good enough to proceed! Occasionally, I am guessing chemo did not happen because the doctor had judged the process to be ineffective. To realize that a familiar face was missing on occasion was always sad and sobering.

In a few minutes the nurse would return with an even bigger smile and a packet of needles, bags, gloves and anti-nausea drugs. These were my signal that all systems were "Go" and the chemo would begin. A note about chemo: I had never seen a need to be educated about this process because I had never planned to have cancer. We learned quickly that chemo is a very precise drug with a particular chemical formula designed for each individual patient. The product is not even concocted until the lab report comes back, because the medication is extraordinarily expensive and would be wasted if for some reason it could not be administered to the designated patient. Before treatments were explained, I had chemo formulas in the same bottle as an aspirin or an antacid. Not so!

Just prior to the administration of chemo, a lovely "cocktail" of drugs (not my terminology, for sure) is given for protection against tummy issues. These are administered both through infusion and orally. I was blessed to never become ill from the chemo. Some people endure a huge amount of upset even with the precautionary drugs. As I understand, the pre-treatment drugs are increasingly being improved and they are becoming more effective for more patients. Roger usually got us each a cup of coffee and at some point a nurse offered us our choice from a basket of snacks provided by the center.

We found the nurses skilled and attentive and always ready to answer our questions. We had been blessed in finding this very special place. I would guess that all cancer centers are great, but a special connection seems to develop with the one to which the patient is connected. We could have chosen a center a few minutes closer to home, but neither of us would have changed a thing! The driving force was the fact that this was the center connected with my health record, and we were content and blessed.

I believe that we spent four to five hours at the center on most chemo days. Those days always included both radiation (usually completed first) and chemo treatments. Some days, Roger would spend some time walking around, maybe even going outdoors for a bit, but I remained tethered to the process. I was always grateful that he could move around. We carried a bag packed with magazines and books to the center although we rarely looked at them. A special friend and her husband had provided the beautiful bag filled with goodies that were appropriate for the hours in chemo. This time was just special to be together. I once again remember that Roger spent much of it holding my hand.

One thing still amazes me about the chemo experience. Rarely did I have even an inkling of fear or dread as that egregious process began (except for the single difficult needle stick). Realizing that the Lord enables, I do understand the source of the strength and peace; however, I had braced myself for the worst possible emotional reaction even though I had prayed. I must admit that I was always amazed by the Lord's working, and the courage that I felt was not from within me. It was God!

I do best if I am absolutely certain of both process and outcome and I had no certainty in either of those areas this time. I believe that I became a bit weepy for a few minutes one day, and I nearly had a meltdown on moving day (more about that next), but beyond that, we meandered along the path that we had been set upon. God is the only source of whatever strength we have had including during those hours when the chemo was literally flowing to its designated target. I am reminded of the words of a hymn writer: "How can I say thanks," a wonderful hymn that ends with the words, "To God be the glory for the things He has done."

A few words about the wisdom of embracing chemo seem appropriate. I have known people who have done chemo once and said they would never do it again. There are still others who refuse to even consider it the first time. For us, the issue was simply one of trust. While we were not excited about the prospect of chemotherapy, we believed that the Lord had allowed medical science to make some marvelous discoveries and we understood that they may not work well in particular situations. The truth, however, is that we were blessed with a peace that I should follow my doctor's orders. We believed that God had especially chosen Dr. R to direct us in this recovery path.

We trusted our medical team completely, so for us, that was the answer. I believe it is absolutely necessary for each of us to bathe our friends in prayer when they have such a decision to make, and then we just need to support them completely in their conclusions. And I respect the fact that some may not agree with our philosophy, choosing to question every move of the doctor.

Two things helped us in this area. We did go to a second opinion appointment at Johns Hopkins Hospital in Baltimore, and our radiologist pulled up a detailed protocol that showed the oncologist's plan as a very wise one. Never be afraid to ask for a second opinion. In fact, Dr. R. encouraged us to go to Hopkins, and even had the appointment scheduled for us. We met with the chief doc of lung cancer who concurred completely with our doctor. The matter of trust is as personal and difficult as the disease itself. For each of us, the Lord Himself is the best advisor, and He may work in different ways from one person to another.

Two days (out of seven weeks total) in chemotherapy were especially tough. The first was the day that my port refused to work. The second was the day that we were all moved from the lovely cheerful room full of windows to another area that seemed sterile and which would deliver the chemotherapy in what seemed to me to be a darker and gloomier surrounding. The second room seemed to scream of terrible illness and doom, and neither of us wanted to think of that as remotely possible.

After several attempts to access the port on the second day of treatment, finally the needle was placed. The pain on that day had been incredible, despite the fact that the port's purpose was to ease all of the potential discomfort. My sister and my special prayer warrior friend had determined to be with me, and I am sure my sister endured much pain as she held my hand and I squeezed hers. I believe this experience redoubled Roger's desire to always be my support and driver from that point on if it was chemo day. By the way, some people are able to have chemo and drive themselves. I had nothing to do with that decision because Roger had immediately determined that I would not travel alone. And I must confess that I enjoyed the company and came home rather tired. His decision was likely not only sweet, but also wise!

When we went in for chemo week three, there was more bad news about the dastardly port. It had moved itself and breeched the skin. My nurse explained the possibility of infection and recommended with unquestionable firmness that we needed to go back and see the surgeon who had placed it. An appointment was made for that same afternoon and off we went. The bad news was that there was definitely an issue; the good news was that it could be fixed… by another surgery where the current port would be removed. A new one would be placed on the opposite side of my chest. If you are counting, that's an incision on each side, all in the space of one more brief surgery. The incisions were small, but when they are on one's body, their size doesn't mean much.

This "event" was simply a quirk that happens sometimes, and it was not a fault of the good surgeon nor had I done something to cause it to rupture through the skin. Surgery was scheduled for the next day. From that point, there continued to be some minor problems getting the needle in place, but it always did find its way in. I must keep the port for a while yet, and that necessitates having a solution flush the internal line on a monthly trip to the center to keep it clear and clean. I am now blessed with a topical numbing agent that I glob on the area an hour before I see the tech, and there is no pain. I use a really big "glob." Thank you, Lord, for this medication.

The second difficult issue was moving day. Let me tell you about that experience. That was the most difficult and challenging day in chemo, the day when I clearly spun out of control and found myself in need of much support, even beyond Roger's presence. I believe several of the staff called what I experienced a "meltdown," and they even assured me that my behavior was in the normal, expected and acceptable range for the circumstances. I know the Lord was scrunched up in that chair holding me… but when we ignore His presence, He doesn't necessarily push for recognition. I don't use the word stupid, very often, but ignoring His presence is definitely not a bright option to exercise!

The original room where we had spent the first three weeks in chemotherapy was bright and the windows looked out on a beautiful garden. I could almost forget about the cancer when I was there. Someone, however, decided that the lovely room should be remodeled, and so we were moved to a smaller and darker room where curtains separated all of the patients. I could see very little of the nurses' activities, and I felt that we were so isolated from everyone and everything else in the room. I do not know what precipitated my reaction, but I would have to say my humanity reared its ugly head. I cried uncontrollably and even Roger could not bring comfort. Whoops!

Looking back, I believe the aura of the room probably frightened me. It screamed of illness and death and I had not had that experience in the original room. I believe every nurse and every tech who had ever dealt with me came quickly to hold my hand and reassure me, and in time the Lord settled me back down. News travels fast in a cancer center! I was embarrassed and wished that I could have crawled out of the room, but practicality dictated that I would get up, pass other patients who had probably been unnerved by my audio performance, and walk out of the room when treatment was complete. The one good that came at that time was that I learned there was one window in this area and the nurses decided it may be good for me to have a window seat for future treatments. From that time on, I did enjoy the beauty of the parking lot (my new outside world), and just being able to see the outside world seemed to have a calming effect for me.

Perhaps, for me the problem of pride is greater than it is for others, but therein was most likely the worst of the ordeal. I was totally embarrassed by my behavior and would have given nearly anything to have been able to wipe said performance from everyone's memory. Foolish, huh? The issue was complicated by my desire to have an impeccable testimony for the Lord, and I saw this entire shenanigan as a terrible blot on my record.

Life goes on and I found myself more than ready to adjust and move on. A wonderful lesson came through this time; pride does, indeed, go before a fall. God, however, is never finished with us if we want Him to use us, and He will fix the mess we have made and restore us to usefulness. Further, pride is definitely a reminder of our need to repent if we will only listen for the prompt! Thank you, again, for loving us so much, Lord! And thank you for gently helping me to learn to live in your grace instead of to a standard that I have set for myself.

LESSONS LEARNED

- ❖ Even though we may be correct in assessing our own faith as deep and committed, real faith is often most tested, developed and obvious when circumstances become what would be considered as fearful and unexpected.
- ❖ When God takes us into a dark room of existence, He never fails to go with us, and He desires to make His presence known.
- ❖ When we have "meltdowns" and other kinds of failures, He is most capable and ready to pick us up and surround us again with His love.
- ❖ In daunting times such as during chemotherapy or radiation, a well-thought out, God-directed plan of attack is wise. Hymns and spiritual songs are great! I wish I had thought of and rehearsed that idea as the meltdown was occurring!
- ❖ In situations where our lives are necessarily placed in the care and control of others, befriending them and praying for any expressed needs as well as for their dealings in our particular situation is a special privilege.
- ❖ Regardless of how desperate any situation seems, God has the ability to "fix" the situation according to His will. He will even pick us up from our prideful falls and restore our souls. Seems like this is an ever-repeated and beautiful lesson!

CHAPTER VIII
EXCITING MOMENTS IN THE MIDST OF UNCERTAINTY

"Be not afraid of sudden fear… For the Lord shall be thy confidence, And shall keep thy foot from being taken."
Proverbs 3:26

The verses above are from Proverbs 3, and their promises can be of such great power as He reduces those fears that could have been overwhelming. Realizing that the Lord was doing something of great value in my malignant life helped me to relax through the treatment process. Not having an idea of what is ahead is, at the very least, daunting! Truly, this faith was a special blessing. Just today when we saw Dr. R. for a regular monthly appointment, he made the comment that he would be "very concerned about any patient who had NO fear."

I love the second half of Proverbs 3:25: "and shall keep thy foot from being taken." I remember the sudden jolt when my foot flew in the air and I crashed to the ground in Tennessee. Even if there is physical hurt, He wants to guide us and protect us. I can still imagine that shortened and dangling leg and foot as the truth of the fall became clear. I ask myself how often the Lord's intercession in each of our lives has kept our metaphorical foot from slipping. So many situations become so much more manageable in each of our lives simply because of His intervention in what He already knew to be the plan.

He worked on our behalf as such an awesome presence on multiple occasions. I want to encourage us all to remember the times in life when, perhaps, the Lord's presence was far greater than anyone could have imagined possible. In His grace, He is often busy in a particular area of our lives and we are not even aware of His activity. Thank you, Lord, for the Holy Spirit who leads us in such moments to the place where we need to be.

Uncertainty is a powerfully appropriate adjective to describe the weeks in cancer treatment. The Lord, however, orchestrated so many beautiful moments during this time, and it seems appropriate to describe some of them in detail. If we are Christians, we all experience those times when we are absolutely "wowed" by the way God orchestrates events in our lives. They often burst on the scene at exactly the perfect time to remind us of His love and power. Some of the events to follow will be new to your reading. A couple of them, I am choosing to elaborate upon from their mention in previous chapters because they were "elephants in the room" for us; perhaps our experience will benefit someone else.

Hair or No Hair?

The management of the entire "hair or no hair" issue actually began months before we even knew that we might have such a question. God was already directing me as I found a very special hairdresser about six months before our cancer storm arrived. The woman who finds one hairdresser with whom she can trust her "crown of glory" throughout her life is truly blessed, but to find a hairdresser of such permanence is rare; most of us wander, from time to time for whatever reason, to find a new one. My finding the perfect one for the pending storm is a pretty neat story. She truly was a God-send well before we knew there would be this little chemo issue!

Early in 2013, when my hairdresser moved her shop to another town, I was on the hunt for someone new. I am not an every week person at the beauty shop, and a small and quiet shop is still my goal for infrequent visits. That style is simply my comfort zone. Quite by God's leading, I believe, I found a hairdresser who had a small shop down a little country lane just minutes from our home. I called and made an appointment and awaited the designated date when I would meet Judy.

As I walked quietly into Judy's shop, there was something a bit odd. There were wigs everywhere; some looked pretty and normal while others were strange in style or color (like blue, pink or orange) or both. There was a day when many of us older saints had at least one wig, but that was in the mid-twentieth century. I began wondering if Judy was still styling in that era, so I asked her about the wigs. Her answer was a beautiful testimony and quite a surprise. Her answer is the catalyst for her becoming the perfect servant to my need.

First of all, she made it clear that she was a believer, and she shared how the Lord had taken her husband as the result of a cancer journey only a few years earlier. I believe he was only forty-two, and he is now in Heaven. The result of her experience with him was that she developed a passion to help other cancer patients. She had felt led to combine her hair-dressing skills with this new passion, and she had become a local "go to" person for ladies facing unsought baldness. She was compassionate as she explained that she had shaved more than enough female heads and she had become skilled in counseling these dear ladies and in recommending the best way to face the coming battle. Fortunately, this young woman, young enough to have found anger at God as the way she would choose to handle widowhood at such a young age, did not follow that path.

I listened intently to Judy's story as she worked her magic on this normal visit, and I found that there was an immediate connection with her because we both loved some aspect of women's ministry. In fact, she had recently returned from a mission trip and was already preparing for a trip to Russia in a few weeks. As she shared her story, I sensed the peace and calm and courage that made her glow, and I knew there was a lesson to strengthen my life. Before I even knew I would need her cancer-aiding skills, God had already set her in my path.

Fast-forward six months. My cancer had now been diagnosed and the ominous possibility of hair loss loomed often in my mind. The oncologist had explained that I would definitely be in the bald group because of the one particular ingredient that was in my chemo formula. I tend to move forward as quickly as possible in crisis, so I knew I needed to seek help in dealing with this situation. What a comfort to know that I had met and become beauty-shop-chair-friends with this dear woman. Walking into her shop and trusting her judgment as I entered crisis mode concerning impending baldness were easier steps because I felt like I knew her. Tonya, my "Encourager-in-Chief" would be in that much needed role for this trip.

Encouragement from a good friend is a bonus in difficult times, and Tonya and Judy had become wonderful friends.

Two incredible happenings made this counseling visit an obvious God moment. These may seem insignificant, but my head was about to lose all of its hair! I simply dreaded living with baldness. For me, each blessing was further evidence that the Lord was walking this journey ahead of us. First of all, Judy explained that a time may come when we must cut or shave this treasured possession, but she did not believe this was the time. Yeah! I had jumped that hurdle… or had I? Only time would tell.

I remember Tonya's words early in this journey: "The Lord and I have had a conversation about this issue, and you are not going to lose your hair." Tonya does not have the gift of prophecy so far as I can tell, but she does have unshakeable faith in the power of prayer. I believe the Lord did intervene on my behalf to address the desires of my heart, even though the baldness issue was not truly significant in the grand scheme of things. It certainly wasn't the major issue in this potentially life and death issue, though I had still managed to capitalize on it!

Secondly, Judy showed me many ways to tie scarves that would hide the baldness and she taught me how to properly wear wigs. She told us about a program from the American Cancer Society that would teach me how to wear light makeup and look the best that I could no matter what was (or wasn't) under the scarf. Having never worn much makeup, I would never have gone to such a program except for the contagion of excitement shown by both Judy and Tonya.

The coming "Make Bev Beautiful" event (intended to divert attention from the head) was made even sweeter when Judy invited Tonya to join me for the program. I was beginning to feel more comfortable with the new look that seemed to have been dictated for my future. By the way, there are many (free) programs offered in local communities for cancer patients. Oncology centers provide a wealth of information where these are concerned. One of the best things a cancer patient, male or female, can do is to explore the programs that are available.

Now here is a piece of advice about chemo hair loss that Roger found... probably on the internet where you can believe anything. He was adamant that I needed to follow this advice and so I did. As I think back, I believe it may have provided some protection from the ominous diagnosis. He had read that a chemo patient should be very careful and treat the hair with the following process: limited shampooing and only with baby shampoo, absolutely no other hair products, and no blow dryer. You can imagine that I was not the most gorgeous head of hair in the church or wherever else I went. I had learned to gently brush through my hair as it dried and that did give it a bit of body.

I am fairly certain that dreading hair loss put me with the great majority of women (and some chemo-inflicted men) who have received this dictum. I believe that God, because He is God, exercised His privilege to grant my heart's desire. He works such miracles often in the lives of those who love Him, although for those who walk this journey and do not see such a miracle does not mean that He is absent. He is still very much present, working uniquely in each of our situations.

Sadly, I must admit that I did not make this blessing easy for the oncologist. Every week during the brief oncology visit, I reminded Dr. R. that I still had a full head of hair. I always took the opportunity to credit the Lord with this "miracle," the doctor shrugged nonchalantly, and the visit progressed. On a really good day, he would remind me that we still had weeks to go! These precious moments of God's presence in our lives come, not because of our goodness but as the result of His grace. I know I had done nothing to deserve this special favor. Thank you, Lord, for your special grace and mercy.

To every woman who has gone through this experience and lost her hair and to every woman who may face such a trauma in the future, He is able and He will sustain you! I am so grateful that I am not giving you firsthand experience about baldness, but despite my head of hair, I can encourage you. He is God and He is always walking ahead of us. I have so much admiration for the women who have walked this dreaded no hair path, especially when they have completed the walk courageously and with beauty and grace that can only come from above.

The Challenges of Radiation

Briefly, I want to share a couple of warnings that came our way early in the treatment process. These two actually relate to radiation. From my dad's radiation experience and from talking to others, it was no surprise to be cautioned that there may be some burning and that the degree depended on several variables. "Not to worry," the nurse said. "There are wonderful lotions and creams to ease the pain of a bad burn."

I prepared mentally for such a burn and we pled with God that it would not come. By the end of radiation, I had a small spot that was a bit of a challenge. There was, however, no major and severely painful burn! Fortunately, the creams and lotions worked well; if one seemed to lose its power, another one was quickly supplied.

A further caution was that because of the location of the radiation, I would suffer from the most extreme sore throat imaginable. The esophagus is located so close to the radiated area that there would be no way to avoid this pain. Again, I was comforted with the promise that there would be a drug that would bring some relief, albeit limited! And again, God was so gracious. I did not have either a major or a minor sore throat. In fact, there was NO sore throat. Thank you, Lord, so much for being the Great Physician!

I expected that radiation would be a lengthy procedure with all of the pre-positioning and whatever else may need to be done. I attribute the experience in this area to the way Wellspan and the Gettysburg Center have organized themselves. I rarely waited five minutes before my name was called to have that treatment. When I walked into the treatment room, everything was set up and usually within fifteen minutes, I was walking out. If it was not a chemo day, I was quickly headed home.

Happy Anniversary?

Forty-seven years of marriage isn't the textbook milestone (like twenty-five or fifty, for example), but every anniversary is so special. We had spent the last forty-six anniversaries in any number of ways, from brief trips to a special surprise party at the forty mark to a quiet evening at home; we have never taken a cruise or done any of the "wow' trips. No event was ever extravagant, but all were special. We especially enjoyed the surprise backyard picnic with our closest friends for our fortieth! The quiet, no frills plan is simply our preference.

June 24, 2014 would be quite different because of our circumstances. Not only would we show up at the cancer center for a 9:00 A.M. radiation appointment, but wouldn't you just know… this was the week's day for chemo. Thus, we would be at the center for a good portion of the day. We were several weeks into the treatment process, so we both understood that I would be predictably tired by the time we arrived back home. We resigned ourselves to this special day being the quietest anniversary we had ever spent. And the truth of the matter is that the reality check that comes with a cancer diagnosis made us so content simply to have the day together!

To say that we were not prepared for the sight that would greet us when we entered the center that day would be a wonderful example of understatement. As I think back, I believe the receptionist for the building who sits just outside of the cancer area had a particularly curious smile that day. Every day, walking into the center brings a host a familiar faces among the patients, but each day there are also some new faces added. On this particular day, when we walked in, everyone began clapping… those who at least knew us by face recognition and those who did not! This day would turn out to be far more exciting than we had ever guessed.

A large bouquet of balloons, anchored to the counter by a bag of Hershey kisses, greeted us. There were a multitude of posters that I believe the center receptionist had made; they were all over the reception room. Radiation was short and sweet, as usual, but entering the infusion center was a different story. My chair was decorated with balloons and a "Happy Anniversary" sign. The nurses were almost as excited as we were, and of course, throughout the day, patients coming in would wish us a happy anniversary.

A highlight came at the end of the day when another couple walked across the room to talk with us. She had been tethered to infusion lines just as I, and they had come not only to wish us a happy anniversary, but also to explain that this was their anniversary, too. Because they appeared to be somewhere close to our age, we were surprised when they told us they had been married for nineteen years. My immediate thought was that they had been widowed, but the man's explanation changed that idea. He said, "It took us previous marriages to 'get it right,' but we are happily married now."

Our new friends pulled up two chairs and we continued to visit even after I was unhooked from chemo. In fact, we remember getting the idea that the center was ready to close and it was time for us to disappear. Our children had orchestrated a happy occasion despite circumstances. Truly forty-seven became one for the books!

How Many Thousands of Dollars for the Medicine?

You may remember that the doctor told me on the last day of radiation and chemotherapy that I would be on no extra medicine. And to the best of everyone's knowledge, that was true. A CAT scan several weeks after treatment, however, showed tiny cancer nodules were still in each lung. That was troubling and the doctor explained that the solution was either more chemo or palliative care for what he predicted would be the remaining four months of my life I wasn't truly inclined in either direction. Just as a side note, that doctor visit was one week before Christmas in 2014. Merry Christmas, for sure!

That evening, just after dinner, the phone rang and it was Dr. R. He said, "I may have some good news for you." He told me that gnomic testing had been completed early in my treatment and the result was that I had one of three mutations that are sometimes associated with lung cancer. In fact, I had an ALK mutation, and there was a specialty drug that had been recently approved by the FDA, especially and only for the ALK mutation. If I were willing, we would do all of the preliminary work and I would begin the drug. Forthrightly, he explained that this was not a cure, but it may extend my life a bit. I signed up, almost without even looking to Roger for approval. One thing I knew was that we both were praying for more years together, and we were continuing to trust the Lord for that hope and dream in whatever way He chose to work.

Fast forward a few days to the time when the insurance company called to say that they had received the scrip for my new drug. Total cost: more than $200,000 per year. The good news, according to the company was that we would only be responsible for about one-third of the cost. I suddenly felt as if I were in a fast-moving car and someone had just slammed on the brakes! Roger immediately suggested that we would sell the house if we had to do so. The only problem was that the house is lovely, but modest enough to bring, at best, a couple of years' worth of our share of the payment. And where were we to live if we used that solution and faced the loss of our home?

We prayed and realized we were helpless to even get any counsel at this hour, so we spent a quiet evening and a fitful night, and we called Stacey, our new best friend at the cancer center the next morning. She is the center expert on all things financial, and she assured us that things would be worked out and she asked us to be patient through the day as she searched for answers. To make a long story short, in about half an hour's time, I had become the recipient of a scholarship from a foundation whose only purpose is to help people in severe illness with insurmountable costs. Once again, God had moved a mountain, and He left in its place a ZERO co pay! ONLY GOD could orchestrate this blessing, and we will be forever grateful to Stacey for her continued support in this area.

The financing for this drug will continue to be a concern as foundation funds from one group come to an end, making it necessary to look elsewhere for help. What a blessing that there are those people who work tirelessly to make such drugs obtainable. When the time comes to search further, our friend Stacey at the Cancer Center will again work tirelessly on our behalf. And we will praise the Lord yet again for a very special work on His part in our behalf.

His Word is Perfect!

The blessings so far have been somewhat of a tangible nature. The last one that I desire to share with you here is absolutely the most significant. That is because it falls in the spiritual category… which makes it the epicenter for growth, challenge, and encouragement in any circumstance for every believer. God's Word, profitable in every way to our lives, stands as the greatest of all blessings.

Experiencing God Day-By-Day by Henry and Richard Blackaby was a devotional book of paramount importance through this journey. This book had been a Christmas gift from a friend, and it turned out to be the perfect present to lead me deeper into His presence as it joined my Bible as ever-present help throughout the storm ahead. One of the challenges of the treatment period was the inability to accomplish much physically. That fact, in turn, provided the gift of a lot of reading time. I thank the Lord that He had implanted a desire for me to spend most of that time in the Word, and my special devotional book. Because I am a reader, I read other books, as well, but these two were my definite favorites as I sat on our deck in a swing or a lounge chair and read and read and read. And as He always does, God blessed and blessed and blessed His Word to my heart in many special ways. It was throughout this time that I truly learned how to meditate on Scripture.

I am not particularly proud that I was in my seventieth year when this lesson about meditating on the Word became engrained deeply in my heart, but confession is good for the soul. One does not teach a Bible class in a Christian school without reading and studying the Word. I taught the Word to high schoolers for three decades, and I read and studied faithfully… to be a good Bible teacher and to honor the Lord. And the Lord blessed my heart through the study. How different, though, to have one's mind free and clear of any purpose except that He would "speak to my heart!" What a blessing when we, by design, meditate on the Word and let the Holy Spirit mine its truths into our very being.

While it should never take the place of the Word of God as it is spoken into our hearts and lives, a good devotional book is often helpful. And here is where another very special blessing from the Lord began to happen. As days of special need or possible stress would approach, I found myself turning to the page in this devotional book that had a Scripture verse and meditation for the particular day that caused some concern. Often, I was jumping ahead to a date weeks or even a couple of months ahead of the present day because of an event that had pressed a bit of concern into our minds. Incredibly, every time I turned to a special date for comfort or encouragement because I knew what was ahead on the schedule for that day, the verse listed was exactly perfect for the situation. These "jump ahead and be comforted" verses truly brought peace and comfort in the most perfect way.

God continues to work in the area of directing our minds to appropriate Scripture. Recently, after a particularly stressful morning with an insurance issue, I volunteered at the hospital for the afternoon. I was in a bit of a kink! Immediately noticing that the spin rack of Christian books had some new items, I stopped to peruse them. My eyes fell upon a women's devotional book and I picked it up and randomly opened it. I prayed quickly as the book fell open, asking the Lord to once again provide a special verse of comfort that would carry me through the afternoon. Are you ready? I was looking at Psalm 46:10: "Be still and know that I am God." Immediate calm swept over me as once again, as God had given me the perfect meditation for the imperfect time I faced. Sometimes, the verses are the old favorites as this one was, but the Holy Spirit has gone through the catalog of our memorization of the Word, and He delights to pull the perfect one to bless us! At other times, He gives us verses new to our attention. God loves to honor His Word into our lives!

There are many other areas where I could share God's perfect blessings. I present these few simply that you might rejoice and be reminded of how much He cares for each of us. What a blessing that whatever is important to our lives is His concern, as well.

LESSONS LEARNED

- ❖ Our lack of confidence can become a wonderful opportunity to see God's wonder-working power, His strength, and His grace in action.
- ❖ He is our Rock and Fortress and ever-present Help in time of trouble.
- ❖ He will bring circumstances and people together to minister in our lives, even when we have no clue what is truly happening.
- ❖ As we stay close to Him in prayer and Bible study, He will provide exactly what or whom we need precisely when needed.
- ❖ It is so special when, sometime in the future, we can look back over past weeks or months or even years and see how He was working to prepare us for the place where we found ourselves at a later time.
- ❖ There are lessons and miracles, awesome moments of God's intervention on our behalf, often. We need to always trust that He may work in ways far above what we could ever ask or think.

CHAPTER IX
YUCK! I AM STUCK IN A TROUGH!

"O Lord, God of my salvation, I have cried day and night before Thee."
Psalm 139:5

Knowing what new calamity may strike and when it will strike could be considered as tasks of most difficult, if not impossible proportions! My worst judgement would proclaim to the world that in God's grace and with the earnest prayers and the gracious help of family and friends, I sailed through the cancer journey with peace beyond comprehension, no matter the nature of the latest calamity. None of the possible negative challenges ever touched my life and all was good. I carried an award winning smile, no matter where I went, and people were always blessed by my presence. My umbrella was complete protection from the assaulting storm clouds, and I was sailing well above the storms. Those are the statements I would love to make with utmost integrity.

Now for the truth. As I have already stated, this journey has sometimes been a challenge. In fact, there have been a few times when circumstances seemed difficult to a ridiculously exponential factor. That the Lord was with us at every juncture and that we relied on His power and that He always enabled… all of that is true. In addition, however, despite my proclamation that I was not afraid, I now understand that I often was at least a little. While I would like to think that everyone loved my presence at all times, there were countless moments when I am sure that no one would have found much joy in my being. In fact, there were times when I am not sure how those who were closest to me even managed to stay near! Despite the fact that I proclaimed strength, there have been times when I have been very weak. Nearly every Sunday, our pastor admonishes the congregation to "stay in the Word." When we are not completely in step with our Lord, disastrous results often come our way… and sometimes, I fear that I have been the perfect image of disaster.

The tornadic activity that spewed from my being, simply by a quiet assault of words sometimes, must have been so difficult, especially for Roger and my family, to endure. The truth and power of God's Word, however, as it billowed around me and in the midst of the clouds was the greatest possible evidence of a true and living and loving God Who was always present. He gave such a sweet presence to those who endured my calamities as they protected me from my self-invented storms.

"Stuck in a Trough!" That's quite a title for a chapter that is swallowed in the midst of so much joy and rejoicing much of the time, even when the torrential winds were assaulting not only my body, but all of our emotions as well. And yet, writing about the down times is important if you are to be encouraged for the storms that may come, either as in a whirlwind or ever so gently as an April shower, into your own life. Even an April shower, when it is our own, can seem like a torrential downpour if we fail to embrace the Lord. Knowing that our Lord is with us no matter how we may seem to be failing is a blessing beyond compare. Yet, there are times when we consciously or unconsciously determine to walk on our own power, days like my moving day experience.

It is never God's desire that we be stuck in the muck and mire; yet, He may allow us some of those experiences just to sharpen our faith in His power for our lives. The prodigal son found himself eating from a trough, but when he realized the error of his ways, his father greeted him with loving arms and complete forgiveness. What a blessing that our Heavenly Father designed that attribute for us through the forgiveness of our sins secured by Jesus Himself.

Further, He may desire to teach us lessons that we may otherwise never have learned.   And then He will gently lift us back onto the dry, yet fertile ground and sunny skies as He chooses. The Apostle James warns believers that there will be times of testing. Jesus Himself reminds us that life is not always sweet in its circumstances. A smile comes to my face as I tell you unswervingly that He is able, and the trough is never too deep for rescue if we are trusting in Him. Trough experiences carry with them the possibility of even greater impending disaster, and our comfort is in His presence to guide us back to dry ground.

My journal became a source of expression for the tough times, and today, I am so joyful that I can go back and read them and be reminded of where I sometimes was. Truly, I was not thankful for most of those "trough" times, but they were still a way for me to be even more aware of the mountaintops. The mountain top experiences would probably not seem quite so special if it were not for the comparative depth of the valleys.

My journal actually became a public document of sorts, at least to family and close friends. Never confuse journaling with the teenaged years when you wrote to "Dear Diary." I found that I was often expressing thoughts that I truly wanted the special people in my life to understand. Most journal entries were positive and that was a good thing. Sometimes I was unable to speak the words of whatever my mind and heart wanted to say to others, but I found that I could write those thoughts!

My journal often lay on the coffee table in our family room, and I consistently suggested that friends and family were welcome to pick it up and read. I honestly do not know if anyone ever did read any of its pages, but it was certainly there as a testimony to anyone who desired. It remains accessible to anyone who is interested today. I continue to journal almost daily and I highly recommend the process as great fertilizer for spiritual growth.

Perhaps a look at a few of the more painful journal entries will help you to understand our plight through my eyes on the most difficult kinds of days. So here they are. This "gut level" sharing of trough times is not easy, but my prayer is that you will see that God's strength is as available in our weakness as in our times of strength. Coupled with the rest of our story, these weak times truly, eventually, became points of victory. Parenthesized words are my current comments and assessments about the entry.

- ❖ March 21: "Dr. B called to say that pathology is back and there is more cancer--- early caught and only a little, but nevertheless, more. (It is overwhelming to guess what is ahead..." Dr. B did not paint any rosy picture; he simply explained that, although he had come from surgery believing we were finished with this nasty and undesired villain, in reality it was still present).

- ❖ May 7: "Death in this life brings the ultimate and highest presence with God." (I share this entry though it sounds positive {and it is}. But I share it because when that awareness that death could be knocking at the door first presents itself, it is overwhelming at the least. While I completely believed what I had written, the reality of death was still, in some ways ominous. I'm a wife and mom and grandma… there's still a lot to experience. It is difficult to face the possible separation from our earthly, tangible experiences despite the glories to come).

- ❖ May 10: "Oh, how I crave the daily presence, peace and comfort that comes from the Lord." (Sounds like it was just a tough day!)

- ❖ May 24: "I am afraid for my grandchildren in all of this. Lord, please grow their faith. Give Spencer, Garrison, Maddi and Mark a special measure of your grace." (Having dealt with students for thirty-five years of my teaching career, I am so aware that while children are resilient, yet they are also deeply touched by crisis).

- ❖ June 27: I am exhausted even though I slept well." (I find comments like this one peppering my journal from this point on, despite the fact that I continue to tell folks that I was impervious to fatigue as this battle progressed. Roger reminds me that I spent much of the summer on our deck in a reclining chair, reading. And I did finish the New Testament and Genesis through Isaiah in the space of that summer. I wonder, was I simply too exhausted to get out of the chair? How thankful I am that the Holy Spirit continually prompted me to pick up the Word. And yet, fatigue can be a trying challenge).

- ❖ July 16: (Last day of treatment): "I feel such a strange sense of loss; I will miss the daily encounters with these medical personnel who have become dear friends." (Lots of tears this day! We had come to respect and love all of those who had been entrusted with my care (and Roger's comfort) in the multitude of hours we spent in treatment and appointments with doctors. Oncology staff are surely called of God for this difficult task, even when they are not aware of the fact. What kind, gentle and sweet spirits they are!)

- ❖ July 18: "Some sharp pain in my hip. Probably from a lot of walking." (Tonya had spent the day with me having a celebratory shopping trip. Probably not the wisest way to celebrate, but definitely what we enjoy).

- ❖ August 7: "I know I need to slow down, and I am having so much trouble doing so. Lord, please help me to accomplish this without the aid of yet another crisis!" (I figured out that sometimes, the only way the Lord can get my attention is through an obstacle and that is NOT fun! Yet, today, a year later, I must still confess to having this problem. I am gifted with this idea that I can do it, and I don't need help. {What pride…ouch!} I wonder how often I have hurt Roger or others by refusing their help when they are trying to be so kind and caring!)

- ❖ October 20 (a year later): "Big lump in my throat this morning. (My mind just races as I await results from the latest CAT scan this afternoon. Roger is very sober and has been since the blood work and scan last Friday. Tonya just called to remind us to call her as soon as we can. This is so hard for everyone).

Roger was so fragile while we waited in the examining room for results. It seemed like time hardly passed… we were stalled and didn't know when the doctor would be in. We received a good report!!! No changes on the CAT scan results from last month. But Dr. R also emphatically reminded us that this cancer will not ever go away. That is hard to hear even though I continue to believe in the power of our Great Physician.

There are always going to be challenges. We need to be read up, prayed up and focused up to the Lord so that we are not caught unprepared. Any state of unpreparedness on the part of us Christians brings a disgustingly huge smirk to the face of the enemy. Surely, that smirk is something we would never want to make possible.

Now a couple of years out from the beginning of this journey, the rough times occasionally continue their assaults, and I desire to share one of those with you. The Lord has been so gracious in bringing recovery. Despite that fact, the times of

CAT scan and blood work re-evaluation can bring tremendous stress.

At this point, every month's protocol is blood work and a visit to the oncologist so that he can interpret the myriad of confusing statistics. In addition, every three to four months requires another CAT scan to see if there is the lingering cancer is in my body, and there are yearly PET scans; of course, these bring comparisons to previous numbers and reports. The possibility always exists that in His divine purpose, God may allow a really nasty test result. That reality, dear friends, can bring stress to any family. The wait for CAT or PET scan reports is difficult, even when we are trusting the Lord. I have talked with several cancer patients who concur with this thought.

Sometimes when we have walked outside of the Lord's power, stress, like an ugly critter that it is, rears a controlling power over our nature. What does that stress look like? Just know it isn't pretty! It may mean tears or unkind, poorly thought-out remarks; for Roger, I believe it simply brings an unimaginable need to cope, not only with the ramifications of a disease but also with a wife who can easily spin out of control. Sometimes, it shows up as a mild kind of depression or sadness, thankfully never yet for both of us at the same time.

We realize that being in the trough has nothing to do with God's will and everything to do with our attitudes which can control our will if we allow them to do so. How should we approach such moments? There's only one thing that is proper. We need to ask the Lord for forgiveness and re-boot our attitudes. I often find that I must purposely and faithfully get back into the Word. What a great and loving God He is as He blesses His Word to our spirits.

Please plant a seed of survival in your heart, should you ever need a re-focus on how the Lord is directing. Slowly and at times a bit painfully, I have been able to yield difficult areas of my life to the Lord. There is that yield word again; sometimes He waits patiently for us to understand His movement and direction in our lives. And as soon as possible, get busy!

About a year ago, I learned of the need for volunteers at our local hospital, and soon it was obvious that here was an area where I could serve in an intentional, yet not "full time Christian service" way. After enjoying a wonderful training day, I was able to be placed in the gift shop where I could greet a myriad of people who passed through. I may never conquer the challenge of a cash register, but I am working at it! And volunteering carries with it a special blessing in service.

I have also had the privilege to teach several home school English courses to small groups of high schoolers that have, each time, included at least one of our grandsons. I loved our discussions of the principles that Shakespeare wove into Romeo and Juliet even though he may have been unaware of the life lessons my students would come to see. And once again, the Lord has opened a door for me to team teach a ladies' Sunday School class at our church, and I adore the opportunities to speak before women's groups on special occasions. Returning to serve in areas that have always been uppermost in my life is so encouraging.

A healthy, God-led re-focus is often the anecdote for trough experiences. Upon the realization that we have fallen into the stinky trough, we must not wallow in the mud. Rather we must escape and GET BUSY for the Lord. He is pleased with our service and the activity is truly a balm in Gilead!

For each of us, the adjustments are different, but when catastrophe of any kind comes into our lives, there will likely be a need for some adjustment. Sometimes the catastrophe is on the slight side in everyone else's perspective, but the truth is that when our own lives are challenged, the challenge will likely appear to be larger than life. Looking back, I realize that there were times when I was a bit short in praising God. My gratitude attitude was sometimes on the shrinky- dink side and the result was unnecessary misery for me and disappointment for my Heavenly Father. These were the times when the trough seemed to open up and swallow my being. I wonder how often each of us would be spared the chasms of life if we would simply choose gratitude and stand up, dust ourselves off and get busy for Him again.

Yes, there will be tough times in any of our lives as we face the road ahead. Our God, however, knows where the potholes, sinkholes and troughs are, and He has a perfect plan to teach us and grow us through them… and He desires that we rise above them. With His help, we never need to wallow in the pigpen of despair!

LESSONS LEARNED

- ❖ God is God and He deserves our praise and thankfulness, no matter what the situation may be.
- ❖ God is a very present help in times of trouble.
- ❖ Trough experiences can make us feel slimy and yucky, but we don't need to stay that way. He always stands ready to clean us up!
- ❖ We need to own the trough times and turn our thoughts positively toward serving others who are not only observers but targets in the pigpen of despair!
- ❖ The pride that keeps us from facing the difficult times and admitting to the struggles is the same pride that keeps us from seeking the help of others.
- ❖ While we do not have to share all of the muck and mire with the world, our spouses, family and a few well-chosen confidants can be an added source of strength for us. I have noticed that when I fall into Roger's arms in tears or fatigue, there is the strength of that three-fold presence: the Lord, my precious Roger and me!
- ❖ When we know that God is in our entire circumstance and we neglect to share the harder times with others, we fail God. We have refused to share His greatness at these difficult points of our lives. We have an incredible opportunity to give thanks and share His power.

CHAPTER X
WHEN TREATMENT ENDS

"The Lord hath appeared of old unto me, saying Yeah, I have loved thee with an everlasting love: therefore with lovingkindness have I drawn thee."
Jeremiah 31:3

Somehow I had concocted in my mind that when the last day of chemo happened, there would be a gigantic celebration and all the difficult events of this catastrophe would be over and forgotten; another part of me wondered what new decisions would be on the docket. And I wondered if life would ever just become the old normal again. Mark it down; uncharted territory comes as much with the end of treatment as with treatment itself. In some ways, leaving the center after the final treatment was akin to being in an open field in the midst of a thunder storm. The question is the same: Where do I go next? The only way forward that made any sense to us was that we needed to be drawn forward by God's power and direction. Faith in that decision, however, did not immediately remove all questions from our minds.

The first question concerned how we would mark this milestone. Many people were rejoicing with us in anticipation of this special day. There would be no huge celebration. Several people had mentioned the need for such a celebration, but somehow, that did not seem to be the style that fit us. We would walk quietly from the treatment center, once again hug in the reception hallway (through a few happy tears) and head home. It wasn't that we wanted to silence the moment so much as that we simply wanted to be silent before the Lord at this time. This was His moment, not ours, because He had allowed us to arrive at this point, and our overwhelming silent praise was all we needed. There would be another Prayer Update that afternoon as so many had prayed us through this day. To the best of our ability, all praise and honor and glory would be given to Him.

Secondly, we absolutely didn't know what to expect next. This phase of the journey is appropriate in some way to anyone who walks any path of catastrophe to its resolution, no matter what that might be. In medical issues, if treatment of any sort is involved, in one way or another, it will end. In fact, the adjustments may be the same even if the situation is far diminished from the "catastrophic" category. What is happening in one's body is always significant to that person and to those who love him/her. A tool box that is equipped for the next phase of the journey would be important.

God's abiding presence was on the top of our tool box. Just as Roger had been physically holding my hand from the moment when I shared the results of the surgical pathology report with him, God had been ever-present, as well. This triumvirate of the Lord, Roger and I has spent much critical time together; we've spent nearly fifty years together, none so critical as the past few. The Lord had walked with us into every medical appointment, He had been present even when Roger could not be (Thank you Lord that the Holy Spirit has no fear of CAT scans and other tests that could play havoc with those of us who are still in the earthly body), and He was deep in my soul through all of the tests and treatments. He rode in the car with whoever was in charge of the daily journey throughout treatment. He held me as I lay on the sofa exhausted after some treatments, and He provided the most beautiful summer to simply sit on our deck and read His Word.

He had heard all of the prayers, silent or spoken by literally hundreds who had prayed, and we believe He was pleased with the worship that flowed as we followed the plan He had given me for the scary times, concentrating on Psalms and hymns and spiritual songs. He heard my silent songs and lists of blessings as I lay on the treatment table. In the darkest of nights when imagination would attempt to gain control (and in fact, sometimes nearly did), He was the Friend Who so often wrapped me in His arms while He gave sweet Roger some much-needed rest. That rest was often illusive, if not impossible for Roger to gain.

He continues to be our guide whether we were headed to a scheduled once-a-month appointment or we are having a "normal" day at home. He is with us, no matter the circumstances. We are learning increasingly to embrace the will of the Father and the guidance of His Holy Spirit in our lives! Many people have implied that our cancer experience is over. After all, chemo had ended, radiation had never caused me to glow in the dark, and we were rejoicing that the daily grind of treatment trips had ended. As we walked from the treatment center for the last time following formal treatment, we should have been walking into a bright and happy sunshine, not a cloud in the sky. Quickly, the new challenges that we would face became obvious.

The first challenge at the end of treatment was... the end of treatment. The gal at the reception desk had become our friend, the girls in radiation knew my body as well as I, the chemo nurses had been through those horrible needle sticks when the port had decided not to accept the needle, and the doctors had become wonderful treatment friends as well as experts and advisors. The truth of the matter is that, although we were all still very much alive and prayerfully on the mend again (thank you, Lord!), the end of treatment was signaled by the daily separation from a group of people whom we had come to love dearly. They were the ones who had greeted us, kept us comfortable during treatment and even celebrated our forty-seventh anniversary with us when we walked into the center on June 24.

We weren't actually saying goodbye forever because I would continue monthly appointments at the Cancer Center for at least the next five years. That daily aspect of the relationship, however, that had grown as we shared a greeting each day would end on this last day of chemo. The dynamics of the relationship change. Multiple new patients would need the same wonderful care that I had received. Choking back tears as I left the chemo chair for the seventh and final time and as I sat up from the radiation table for the thirty-fifth time was difficult. These people had come to mean so much to us!

The morning after the last day of treatment could be likened to driving through dense and heavy fog. For us, that Thursday morning dawned a beautiful July day, weather-wise. We could take our coffee and sit on the deck and relax and not even think about a routine that we had maintained for the last seven weeks. At least in our situation, while this was a wonderful day of rejoicing, it was lonely, as well, in an eerie sort of way. We needed to creatively figure out just what this post-treatment life that the Lord had granted us should look like! How could we best spend this new-found time? Things had definitely changed and some adjustments would be necessary.

Adding to the stark contrast between treatment days and the "new normal" was the answer to a question that I had avoided all through treatment. On the last day, there is a protocol interview with the oncologist as treatment ends. After his assessment of my future as he could guess it prior to a PET scan which would occur in a few weeks, he asked his typical question: "Do you have any questions for me?" He had been cautiously optimistic with us, if you consider the word cautious to mean "Just don't get too comfortable; anything could happen now." Roger and I probably had a dozen questions at this time, but for whatever reason most were not asked.

In fact, I was nearly overcome by this single issue. I had heard of people who had died as a result of their after-treatment protocol. The only thing to do was to blurt out my one desperate question at this opportunity: "What medications will I have to take now?" For the people whom I knew who had cancer before me, I had nearly always heard that there was some kind of post chemo drug treatment. I assumed that fact to be true for everyone. I even knew of one gal who had breast cancer radiation treatment therapy and refused a post-drug regimen. She had opted instead for herbal treatment and she has never returned to the cancer center. And as far as I know, she is doing well several years later. I am fairly certain that I am not so courageous, but if I were, Roger and I had already committed to following doctor's orders, and Roger had become firm on the issue.

The good doctor's answer: "You need no medication." No medication??? That certainly sounded like the right answer, but once again, Satan jumped silently onto my shoulder. He prompted me with such thoughts as "Everybody needs post-treatment meds" and worst of all, "You are probably so bad now that they just aren't going to treat you any longer. You will die, and soon." Coming from the woman who had embraced the Lord's power to heal and who truly believed He would heal, this was not logical thinking.

Another reality of the end of treatment is the change in the treatment status of the patient at the point where he/she lives in community with fellow believers, other friends and neighbors. Throughout treatment, dozens of friends and family were so acutely aware of our circumstances; we know this because someone, it seemed, was always checking on us, and that was nice! After treatment ends, while many continue to pray, cards and calls and visits slow appreciably. There will always be church friends and neighbors who inquire occasionally about the status of the cancer, but those numbers of people will diminish. Perhaps this is a good time to suggest a follow-up inquiry or card on occasion. In fact, an encouragement card even brings a smile to the healthiest of individuals!

Although there are plenty more recovery-mode events, I will mention only one other. Even though there might be return visits for check-ups and port flushes, patients are often told that they are free to live life as they choose. Nothing prepared me for the aches and pains, real and imagined, that would come in the ensuing days. Most recently, we found ourselves in the emergency room with extreme chest pain, jaw pain and arm pain… full-blown heart attack signs. The issue, we believe, turned out to be no more than severe indigestion, but the lung cancer issue blew it well beyond the norm.

The ER doctor explained that radiation in the chest area can make one far more susceptible to heart issues than a person who has never had radiation to the treatment extent. Poking, prodding and testing are far more time consuming and ambitious than the norm and the ER visit groans on and on. While I am embarrassed to admit the fact, sometimes every little ache and pain seems to take on astronomical proportions, now. That is a typical a side-effect of the ugly monster, cancer. I can remember Dr. Geoff cautioning me that such an attitude could develop.

All of these challenges can make one begin to wonder: "Just how do I get back to normal?" Beyond tasks at home, as I have said, for me it was time to get on the move, however the Lord allowed and directed, beyond our walls. The caution here is that we must listen to our bodies and rest, even occasionally giving in when it isn't our first choice.

Recently, a cardiologist observed in some tests that in the area where one third of my lung had been removed, the cavity is totally filled in. We are told that such healing is normal and even happens quickly, but the "fill in" stuff isn't exactly like the old lung that has disappeared. The truth of the matter, however, is that breathing can still sometimes become a challenge. Recovery from shortness of breath happens quickly, but only as I sit down, breath slowly and give myself a chance to recover. That "hole" that filled in did not incorporate new and healthy lung; that is still missing!

As treatment ends and there are decreasing hours each day when I am reminded that I still may have some cancer in my body, I look forward to the time when the ugliness of this disease will no longer plague my body. I am still yearning for that day. Will it ever come? That is simply one of the "take a deep breath" moments that comes when treatment ends. During treatment, it is possible to see each day as one when some degree of healing is taking place. After treatment ends, progress is a bit more vague. I believe the Adversary probably has me on his hit list for frequent reminders so that I may believe the cancer will never leave and that it might even worsen. I am so grateful that through the Holy Spirit, my thinking and my hope are brought back under control.

For every "after treatment" survivor, there is a list of "new normal" standards that is unique to individual taste and talent, physical ability and mindset. The important message here is to do something! God did not intend for us to become couch potatoes (though I spend my fair share of time on the couch); we need to understand that "after treatment" will always be where we now live. We must embrace hope in all that we think and do. He wants us to move on and bring glory to Him for as long as we are able. What a special honor simply to still be on the earth to serve Him

LESSONS LEARNED

- ❖ Daylight is returning and God is still ever-present. He didn't just show up for the crisis; He loves us so much that He was always a part of our lives; His Holy Spirit indwelt me when I was saved as a child, and He never left and He has no plans of leaving… ever!
- ❖ Concentrate on maintaining a grateful spirit and say thank you often.
- ❖ Learning to relax intentionally is important. The mind really wants to keep the body in a state of unrest. With the Lord and the Holy Spirit, we can be the victors.
- ❖ Friends continue to be wonderful allies; be grateful for their support.
- ❖ Begin to look for ways to once again serve others in Christ's name.
- ❖ Remember that with His loving-kindness, He has drawn us and He has incredible plans for the remainder of our lives.

Part Three

A RAINBOW APPEARS

CHAPTER XI
WHAT HAVE WE LEARNED?

"Shew me thy ways, O Lord; teach me thy paths."
Psalm 25:4

We have learned so much about ourselves and about the wretched disease called cancer through the events of the cancer cloud in our lives. As I have stepped back and reread countless journal entries and recounted the events of the journey, I have realized that God has orchestrated the opportunity for a beautiful symphony in our lives. Skies will not always be blue and we will never know what prevailing winds may bring change to us, but we hold tenaciously that joy will always follow grief and challenge. A rainbow will come, and it will even bring the privilege of new lessons that God desires for us to learn!

He has kept us focused upon Himself; He has renewed our joy, sometimes before we even knew it was in desperate need of renewal. He has been our light and our salvation. We treasure the relationship that we have with Him, and we know that He is the source of the positive spirit that has carried us through this time; we would have been incapable of such a spirit in our own power. He has repeatedly shown us that His grace is always sufficient! We have learned that the God who met Daniel in the lion's den is alive and active today, and He has been our God and our strong tower in all times, be they times full of peace or times drenched deeply in the fire of affliction or the pummeling rain from the storm clouds. In the rough moments when we have perhaps moved away from Him, he has waited patiently to woe us back into His presence.

We have learned that in our human selves, difficult and stressful trials have the capacity to diminish our perspective. We may become tired, and then we agonize, and our frustration rears its ugly head. Focusing the journey on Christ and the power of the cross, we can rest in His drawing us back. He aims the rudder in the right direction when we ask for His help; in His grace, He patiently awaits our call to Him. God knows who we are, and there are times when He may allow us to take our own will's path, only to watch lovingly for the perfect time to bring us back to Himself. This is a lesson that, while we went into the journey knowing the principle, struck beautifully as we trusted Him completely for what seemed impossible. You have seen this belief scattered throughout the book; it is evidence of God's faithfulness and it naturally keeps recurring!

Today, I asked that love of my life, Roger, this question: "What have you learned through this little journey?" I was not sure how he would answer, because this time has been so very difficult for him. I am blessed to be the love of his life, too, and he has sometimes endured with great difficulty as he has watched my body default to the various procedures and treatments that it has endured. Just yesterday in our church service, I watched quietly as the words to a familiar hymn seemed to be stuck in his throat and he was obviously reflecting on the past… and the future possibilities.

"Oh," he said, "there are so many lessons." Our lives have truly been blessed in the school of experience. Before the present storm cloud, there had been other sad times, just as in every other family. There have also been the times of joy; so many of those come to our minds that I will just suggest that you spend a few moments worshipping the Lord who always spills some of them into each of our lives. How good it is for each of us to count the blessings. It blesses me to share that as Roger began to recount the lessons learned, it was a long while before he was focusing on the practical. There are so many rich examples that we can cite as spiritual God-moments, and such spiritual moments far exceed those of a more practical nature. Our lists are amazingly similar, too!

One of the first lessons Roger mentioned was the strength from above. When I think about that idea, I am again reminded of how powerfully God has worked in the everyday moments of my life, as well. It is His strength that allows me to stand in our pew and sing the great hymns of the faith (My normal self would spend the entire hymn time in tears). It has been His strength that has allowed me to speak freely about this suddenly cancer-ridden life (My normal self would stand before others in tears, quite likely unable to even choke out a syllable). It is His strength that has given peace about treatment and after-treatment and doctors (My normal self would have agonized through tears, and I likely would never have felt peace about the medical decisions thrust upon us. I am a "fixer" who would have constantly been trying to make things better in my own strength despite absolute certainty that God was in control… and He quite likely had a different and greater plan). Get the picture?

Another lesson that we believe the Lord has emphasized in our lives relates to purpose. Some naturally began asking why such a difficult event was dropped into our lives. We did not choose to ever go there. Remember Joseph? He assured his brothers who had sold him into slavery that they had, indeed, meant their actions for evil... BUT GOD meant them for good. Joseph made this observation on the heels of a massively difficult life experience that had been caused by these same jealous brothers (partly the reaction to his pride). As time has passed from my initial klutzy fall in Gatlinburg, we have learned to say "To God be the glory," no matter what may come. If our hearts have learned to live with God as the foundation, it is more natural to understand that no matter what may come, our lives are all about God and His sovereign purpose.

Have we been stretched? For sure! And sometimes it has seemed the stretching has been beyond our human limits. Many times, especially recently, I have confessed to Roger that I am tired. And he is tired too! We would love to wake up just one morning and make the bed and be able to keep moving. It never fails, however, that I need to rest and catch my breath. We would both love to wake up and go through the day and lay our heads upon the pillows in the evening and realize that we haven't for a moment this day remembered that cancer has invaded our lives and is a most unwelcome guest. As I update what has already been written, I can joyfully say that strength continues to return, even after a couple of years of healing! I smile because we simply have no idea where the Lord will take us next, but we know it will be good simply because He is Who He is!

Twice each year, we see the radiologist and this was one of those days. Dr. Y was on vacation and we had yet another substitute radiologist. It is quite normal that we really appreciate a doctor who bears good news, and we really liked Dr. Substitute this morning.

When we saw our oncologist a few moments later for our regular monthly visit we joked and relaxed as we understood that he cannot say the cancer is absolutely and forever gone. His report was good and we left with his agreement that laughter is a good thing. We have come to understand the deep burden that is carried by any doctor who works with patients, many of whom are terminal. We need to pray for them and ask the Lord to grant them peace.

The Lord is truly riding with us in this cancer cloud, allowing us to have peace and grace in these visits. The lesson learned: these visits may go on for a long time, and that is okay. It is always good to keep a check on cancer, and we do not know how God will use the door that remains open! And another lesson learned in this area: gratitude for medical professionals who truly care for and about each of us needs to be ongoing.

Another lesson learned: God will always use what He has allowed in our lives for us to minister to others. I have a list of more than thirty cancer patients, some of whom I know well. Several on the list are the names of "friends of friends" and I have been asked often to contact them with phone calls and cards of encouragement. How often it has been a blessing to talk to those who are struggling at various places in this storm. The struggle of others who are in some way travelling this cancer road has become real to us!

Let me share just one example of God's ability to work in this area. We changed service providers in a particular area of home maintenance about a month ago. A woman, driving a BIG truck, pulled up for the initial service call. It was a beautiful day and we were drawn into conversation with her. Before either of us knew it, together Roger and I were sharing God's power in my illness.

A month passed and Amy appeared for her second professional visit. When Roger answered the door, she checked to be sure that we were that couple she had been trying to find from last month, and then she asked if she could come in and talk to us. She shared that her husband had been diagnosed (since the last visit) with terminal cancer. He is fifty-four years old, and she was understandably frantic and confused and frightened and full of questions.

God has opened a beautiful opportunity to share not only some things about cancer treatment but also our faith in the Lord through all of this. Our new friend literally wept in my arms and Roger was able to pray for her and her husband before she left. We have already talked with her several times since that visit and we trust the Lord to open whatever doors He chooses.

***A sad update: Amy's husband lived only a few weeks. In that time he professed faith in Jesus Christ and Amy has the peace of knowing she will see him again. We look forward to continuing opportunities to visit with and encourage our new friend.

No cancer in my life? So many privileges to witness and serve would have never happened. The lesson learned is that we need to stay prayed up and in the Word to always be ready to speak of the hope within us both of our salvation and of His working on and in our lives.

And here is one final lesson among the many that could be shared. Frustration will come at times. When you have been busy and active for as many years as my life has spanned, being still, especially when it is because of unsolicited restrictions, is difficult. Family and friends sometimes remind me of how much progress there has been from the initial ominous prognosis. They are so right to remind me, and I must confess, too, that I am often busier than I realize. Activity provided at God's discretion and enablement is a wonderful thing, but the rest He sometimes urges is also very good! Such knowledge is a wonderful help as I seek to continue learning contentment.

No matter the crisis, we will likely become tired and our minds and bodies and spirits will need rest. Joy does come in the morning and it would be a shame to miss that joy when it shows up. God does orchestrate life for each of us as only He knows is best, and He lovingly desires to draw us closer to Himself.

LESSONS LEARNED

- Realizing the perfect control that the Lord desires to have in our lives makes any situation easier to handle.
- Our great God desires every situation in our lives to be used for His glory.
- God desires to teach us something, no matter the situation.
- We will not always understand what God is doing!
- Others are watching our walk; only Christ through the Holy Spirit can make that walk as it should be.
- We will sometimes fail, but He never fails!
- He always stands ready to forgive when we confess our sin. Sometimes it is especially easy to experience sins like ingratitude, and a poor attitude can be especially easy to develop!
- No matter how deep the crisis, it is so small when we view it through the lens of eternity!
- Eternity may be closer than we think! Whether He calls us home through some circumstance that is as individual as we are or should He return to call all believers up to glory, may we be ready.

CHAPTER XII
WHAT'S ON THE HORIZON?

"And I said, O that I had wings like a dove!
for then would I fly away and be at rest."
Psalm 55:6

David was remembering and facing difficult times as he wrote this Psalm. My prayer has been that you would be encouraged by understanding that just like David, all of us face some tumultuous clouds in our skies. We have all had those experiences where we wondered if we would ever again see the light of day. We have times in the shadows when, like David, we would love to simply fly away and be at rest. But the light does eventually dawn! Every day has some challenge, and when the light shines forth from the toughest of those challenges, we sometimes still invent some reason for pause. Perhaps, while we know the Lord has answered, He did not give the result we had hoped would come. Or maybe His timing wasn't what we desired. Even at the end of a difficult journey, questions remain and we must determine to refocus and place our eyes upon His sovereign will.

Just like David, we can have the strength of the Rock. A few verses following the one above, in Psalm 55:18, he stated, "He hath delivered my soul in peace from the battle that was against me…" Before writing, I would have told just about anyone who asked, "This has not been a journey we would have sought, but He has carried us joyfully through." You know, however, that at times the storm clouds have been of major proportion and life has been difficult and joy has nearly escaped us. A keen sense of His perfect presence brings joy, but when we see the hurt caused by our circumstances in the eyes of those we love or even when we are just having a tough day, it is sometimes difficult to see through the fog and the clouds. But God has always been in the midst of the storm! And He stands ready to walk hand-in-hand with us into the unknowns of our future.

We must always remember that while the Lord desires to direct our paths, He will often allow us to make the control choice, and sometimes we don't do so well; most of us do not have a stellar record of following His lead consistently, and we sometimes ignore the "new normal" that He may have chosen for us. I will be forever full of gratitude for His love that always reached to where we were and lifted us back to solid ground. He desires to bring good into our lives.

As I have written, I have found myself recounting the brief times when I wept in Roger's arms as we cried out to the Lord for strength that only He could give. The realization that fatigue and frustration tend to come so easily now is not fun, but it is where life is. Rather than seeing it as a defeat, we are choosing to push forward as practically as possible.

You would perhaps have a similar history. There were no major illnesses or problems other than the brutality that permeates the body during a kidney stone attack… for nearly sixty years of my life. Perhaps sixty is an unidentifiable age at this point in your life, but I would remind you that, should the

Lord tarry, you will quite likely see it far more quickly than you can imagine! And perhaps, like us today, you are well beyond the sixty mark.

Perhaps, you are one of those people who has been fortunate enough and blessed enough to say that you have had no significant physical ills. One of the greatest lessons that we can embrace as we age, whether we be healthy or not so healthy, is to understand that parameters of activity do change for most of us eventually. As we attempt to look beyond the horizon, we are increasingly aware that our pace has slowed and our vision has sharpened. Routine activity that was once paramount now sometimes seems insignificant. Our focus on what can be done for Christ has a new magnitude. And everything is wrapped in the truth of my new abilities (which are a bit less than they were in the past). Victorious living is our standard, no matter what.

It is a rare day when someone does not ask, "So how are you feeling?" I may joke that it isn't the best day, but I am just happy to be here to tell about it. Let me share a post-recovery event that we have dealt with. I am sure that every patient who has dealt with even one surgery or other kind of unexpected challenge would have his own personal list of "tough moments." Keep in mind that some similar experience will likely face each of us at some point, and the significance of our responses in these times cannot be denied.

Keeping Spirits High

The fact that life in some ways seems more complicated a few years out from cancer surgery than it was as we walked before or even through the event may sound strange. I would like to think that those tentacles of cancer that had continually spread themselves within my body throughout the time when treatment was a daily event are now gone, but medically, we simply do not know.

We are incapable to manufacture the peace that we covet, but as the Lord has given us a peace that truly passes all understanding, we have remained true to the belief that the disease will be defeated in this life by our Heavenly Great Physician. We are keenly aware that the Lord could choose at any point to call me (or Roger or you or anyone else) to Heaven, and we know that in His perfect time, that call is the ultimate privilege awaiting every believer. Making clear the fact that our sovereign God may direct any of our lives in an alternative path at any moment is important for us to communicate to others.

We want our non-believing friends to understand that God can do as He wishes and that is good. We want them to hear, even if they cannot comprehend, that we are in a win-win situation no matter what happens next. We want them to know that the Bible tells us that we have an appointed time to be called into eternity. We want them to know that knowing Christ as personal Lord and Savior and having a relationship with Him is the ultimate good that characterizes every believer's life. And we want them to know that they can have the peace of knowing their eternal future is secure.

Being fully aware of the vapor-like quality of our lives may bring both sobriety and challenge. We believe that such knowledge works for our good as we seek to intentionally serve Christ with greater fervency. We all have a bit of tunnel vision and we anticipate our earthly future. Realizing that it will be the highest good in the life of any believer to miss out on some of the earthly milestones that lie ahead is difficult if not nearly impossible to understand. We are blessed with human emotions and the information that a human perspective brings, but He brings peace and a far greater perspective.

Sometimes most of us get so focused on some immediate "Woe is me" moment that we become separated from the "To God be the glory" moments. Most patients and their dear families and special friends can easily identify with this feeling. What a joy to know that at the very moment that we refocus on the Lord, the burden, no matter how heavy, is lifted! It seems to me that sometimes, we anchor our praise and worship in the experiences of a moment rather that in the sheer strength of our eternal Father. We need to be careful to praise the Lord simply and consistently because He is God. And He is God no matter the kind of experience we are having.

If experience alone has become the foundation of praise and worship, that worship will become less meaningful as time passes; and if our praise has been directed solely to His working in the experience, we may land in the mire when we do not experience a "positive" event. Although it is special to focus on WHAT the Lord is doing in our lives, we need to carefully always consider WHO He is, as well. He is… God! We must never forget the catalog of challenges through which He has brought each of us, and while we should always praise Him for the joys He brings in such experiences, our main focus needs to be simply on Who He is.

Where do we go from here? We trust the Lord, thank Him for His grace, purpose and enabling at every turn, and look to the future. Just as the time before crisis, if the Lord brings us to a new normal, we need to see that as the blessing it truly is. Tonya often reminds me that shortness of breath and fatigue are, perhaps, memorials that the Lord has left in my life to remind me, at every turn, that He is my God and my Salvation and He is worthy to be praised. True, the future may be a bit different as the "new" normal sets in, but it continues to be a future for which He has a perfect plan and purpose until He calls me home. Psalm 90:12 reminds us, "So teach us to number our days that we may apply our hearts unto wisdom." What a beautiful challenge, and may it ever be so!

LESSONS LEARNED

- Sometimes David yearned to fly away, and he also yearned for rest. There is a lesson to be learned as we recover, whether it be a physical or emotional or spiritual battle that we have faced.
- Reasonable activity must be pampered with rest.
- Challenges most often accompany recovery
- Learning to weigh our options of involvement becomes very important
- Not being afraid to reply with a gracious "Thanks, but no thanks," attitude may be a true sign of personal growth.
- Understanding the fine line between over commitment, choosing to avoid commitment because it is the right choice, and using recovery as an excuse for not becoming committed can be difficult.
- The Lord must always be a part of our recovery path.

CHAPTER XIII
AN AFTERWORD

"So teach us Lord to number our days that we may apply our hearts unto wisdom."
"Psalm 90:12

Much has transpired since the Cade's Cove hip misadventure. The second hip replacement is doing well, and breathing is ever-so-slightly improved from its original post-surgery condition. Each day brings new opportunities and the ability to spend the time the Lord has allowed in a profitable way.

And there is good news! You have read about updates, and I would like to share two of the most recent ones with you that you may know where we are now. The first is the result of the thyroid needle biopsy, and the second was written after a monthly visit to the oncologist. This visit was ramped up a bit from the norm because it would also include the four month CAT scan report. These reports came in the fall of 2016, a little more than two years after the end of treatment. Might you see God's power and working and rejoice as we do!

~~~~~~~
Update: The needle biopsy: September 29, 2016

"Now unto Him who is able to do exceeding abundantly above all we ask or think, according to the power that worketh within us, unto Him be glory in the church by Christ Jesus throughout the ages, world without end, Amen." Ephesians 3:20-21

Many have experienced God's waiting room for many days simply to receive test results, and the wait is undeniably long! A thyroid needle biopsy was done on September 15, and the results were finally reported today: BENIGN!! I know that the Lord has no more reason to work in my life according to my desires any more than in anyone else's. Yet, He has worked above all we could ask to give this report following the cancer challenge. I remember when I called the cancer event a pothole and then a sinkhole; today the streets are paved with gold. The next hurdle is the quarterly CAT scan in late October, and we are trusting that the report will be as good as the last one when the radiologist did not even call out any nodules. This report will come after a wait of eight days, but that is okay. No matter what, we choose to let God be God; His will is perfect and we will joyfully cling to the old rugged cross. To God be the glory! Thank you for your prayers and concern.

Continuing to rest in His love and mercy and grace and peace,
Roger, Bev, the Smith's and the "Roddy's"

~~~~

Update: The Latest CAT SCAN: October 24, 2016

"Call unto me and I will answer thee and show thee great and mighty things which thou knowest not." Jeremiah 33:3

The verse above is beloved to all believers because it speaks to the power of the Lord and to His desire to work in our lives. And has He ever worked! This morning we had our monthly visit with our oncologist in Gettysburg. Some of you heard our "take" on the latest scan when Roger shared in Sunday School what we thought we saw in the portal report. Now for the official doctor report! Roger and I have learned how to interpret my scans correctly when they arrive in my computer port. According to Dr. R, I am in REMISSION and there is no evidence of cancer. Once again, he explained that he can never pronounce lung cancer as "cured," but we did share with him that we expect many more years unless the Lord returns. My appointments are now moved out to six weeks and can come the same day as the port flush. A few less trips to Gettysburg are a good thing!

We are filled with joy that God would deem it good to give us such a wonderful report, and we are looking forward to what is next on His agenda for us. I never tire of hearing Roger pray for my health and I continue to appreciate your prayers, as well. It is our privilege to pray for all of the needs that we know, and we pray especially for other cancer patients. It is a blessing to have specific ideas of how to pray for the needs of each of you facing this or some other catastrophic problem.

Continuing to rest in His love and mercy and grace and peace, Roger, Bev, the Smith's and the "Roddy's"

> *** As you have seen this closing written, let me explain it. The Smith's" refers to our daughter and her family, and "the Roddy's" refers to our son and his family Otherwise, his family would be "the Hannah's" which might get confused with his dad and me. From the beginning of the updates, we used this closing because we wanted to present the united front that we as a family have presented.
>
> ~~~~~~~~

The most recent CAT scan came just two weeks ago (in 2017), and although it once again came without any message of recurring cancer, there was a glitch. The radiologist noted a blood clot which we had not suspected in the lung. I had noticed within the prior week that my breathing had become an increasing challenge, but the logical assumption was that the medication was causing the issue. We have learned as the result of the CAT scan that such clots are no strangers to those of us who have dealt with lung cancer. Not every patient gets them, but they are common. We trust that, as I write, blood thinners are attacking and dissipating the clot. The best part of this news is that I can now be alerted to the possibility of a future clot if I begin experiencing abnormal breathing issues. Medication will hopefully help me to avoid them.

Life is full of those new horizons, opportunities to work together and separately on the tasks that each of us is provided. There are all the normal chores to accomplish and so many opportunities to be busy beyond our home and to embrace serving the Lord. Our prayer is that we might truly number our days and see them for the blessing and as the gift from God that they are.

It is so easy to squander time, and I suspect we all do that, at least a little. Our goal is to make every moment count in some way. My personal goal is to retrain my thinking so that I always step back and think and evaluate my words and actions mindfully. I need to be sure that this process precedes my actual behavior. I would encourage each reader to evaluate personal goals in the light of God's purpose for your life. After all, He created each of us with distinct gifts and talents, challenges and victories, so that we could live victoriously in the light of His presence.

If we can learn to view every event according to God's will, He will bless! Life is sometimes tough for each of us, but tough does not need to mean utterly impossible. And tough does not always mean catastrophic illness. It may result from deep and unanticipated hurt or from broken relationships or from minor physical issues that we manufacture into crisis. Just as the "fall" of Chapter I made me want to get up and dust myself off, we can often do that with trying times. Grief is natural and it is a process that we must sometimes experience, but we need not remain in that state permanently.

I remember as a child seeing an interesting plaque in a home our family often visited. It said, "Only one life; twill soon be past. Only what's done for Christ will last." Every new dawn presents a golden opportunity to make a lasting impact that honors the God of our creation. Choosing to be as fresh and bright as the sunniest day is a wonderful goal! And therein is true joy.

And one final thought. You may be healthy and in the "prime of life," or you may be walking that road of critical illness. Wherever you are, the Bible clearly promises you one thing. In whichever state we find ourselves, the Lord wants to love on us and bless us. If you will trust Christ and confess your sins and repent and ask Him to come into your life, He will come in. He desires that you may have a deep and personal relationship with Him.

Trusting Him will not only bring you the peace that passes all understanding, but your faith in Him will also assure that Heaven becomes your home for eternity. He will guide your days and gently lead you into Heaven at the perfect time. A beautiful new and perfect life in Heaven~~ eternal life~~ is promised to all who believe. John 3:16 tells us, *"For God so loved the world that He gave His only begotten Son, that whosoever believeth in Him should not perish, but have everlasting* life."

Once again, to God and God alone be the glory forever!

As we continue to rest in His love and mercy and grace and peace, may you, too, rest in Him!